MULTIPLE-CHOICE & FREE-RESPONSE QUESTIONS IN PREPARATION FOR THE AP STATISTICS EXAMINATION

(FOURTH EDITION)

Michael Allwood

D&S MARKETING SYSTEMS, INC.
1205 38th Street Brooklyn, NY 11218

w w w . d s m a r k e t i n g . c o m

ISBN # : 978-1-934780-49-7 / 1-934780-49-9

PREFACE

Welcome to the fourth edition of *Multiple-Choice and Free-Response Questions in Preparation for the AP Statistics Examination*!

This book provides help and support for students as they prepare for the Advanced Placement exam. The first section, "Top Tips for AP Statistics," gives important advice both on a general and a content-specific level. This is followed by "Using the TI-Nspire on the AP Statistics Examination," by Heather Overstreet, where important advice and guidance are provided for students using the TI-Nspire calculator. The third section, "Review Exercises," provides comprehensive questions in all the major topic areas of the AP Statistics course content. These sections are followed by five sample exams, each of which has the same format as the actual AP exam: 40 multiple-choice questions and 6 free-response questions. In each case, as on the AP exam, the sixth free-response question (known as the investigative task) is designed to include ideas a little beyond those encountered during the AP Statistics course.

I strongly recommend – to students and teachers alike – a detailed reading of the Top Tips, as valuable points can be gained on the exam by following the suggestions made there. Additionally, by tackling the Review Exercises, referring to class notes and a textbook as necessary and applying the ideas learned in the Top Tips, the student can build a virtually comprehensive knowledge of the material required for the exam. The practice exams can then be taken either as further review using a textbook and class notes, or under conditions similar to those of the actual test.

In each exam (as in the AP), Section I (multiple-choice) should be completed in 90 minutes, as should Section II (free-response). In Section II, students are advised to spend 65 minutes on the first five free-response questions (Part A) and 25 minutes on the investigative task (Part B). Workspace has been provided for each question, and the tables and formulas that are included on the AP Statistics exam are provided in the last section of the book.

I would like to thank my wife, Anne, for her support and encouragement during the creation of this book. I am also very grateful to my editor, Daren Starnes, whose advice and expertise I greatly appreciate, and to Tammi Pruzansky of D&S Marketing Systems, Inc., who typeset the book and prepared the final copy for printing.

All communications concerning this book should be addressed to:

D&S Marketing Systems, Inc.
1205 38th Street
Brooklyn, NY 11218
www.dsmarketing.com

TABLE OF CONTENTS

TOP TIPS FOR AP STATISTICS

PART I: INTRODUCTION AND GENERAL ADVICE

Introduction

Welcome!

Success on the AP Statistics exam depends on two very important factors. First, you need a good knowledge and understanding of the material in the course. Second, you need to know what is expected of you on the exam: there are particular approaches that are required, and if you're not familiar with these approaches, you are liable to lose a significant number of points.

It is this second factor that we address in the Top Tips. For each section of the syllabus we will look at exactly what you need to do, basing the advice on many years' grading of the exam. And, of course, the idea is that your understanding of the material will be advanced in the process.

Having started with a review of the format of the exam and some advice as to how to approach the two sections, we will proceed with the topics on the syllabus, for each providing a list of the knowledge and skills needed, and following that with the Top Tips.

The Format of the Exam

The AP Statistics exam has two sections: 1½ hours of multiple-choice (40 questions) and 1½ hours of free-response (6 questions), and the two sections are equally weighted. In the multiple-choice section you will receive 1 point for every correct answer and zero for any answer left blank. (There is no longer any penalty for guessing on the multiple-choice section. So, if you are unsure as to the answer to a question, it's in your interest to make a guess.) In the free-response section, the first five questions are designed to take 13 minutes each, and Question 6 should take around 25 minutes. Question 6 will account for 25% of your free-response grade.

There is a break between the two sections of the exam, and calculators are allowed on both sections.

How to do Well on the Multiple-Choice Section,
and on Multiple-Choice Questions in General

You should be aware that multiple-choice questions are liable to confuse you, particularly when you work on them during the course or in the run-up to the exam. Imagine yourself at some point during the year: you have a good but insecure understanding of a topic. You then attempt a multiple-choice question. All of the wrong answers are designed to tempt you – they have that element of plausibility, and so they lead you to doubt the correct understanding that you previously had. And the danger is that this element of doubt will linger on at the back of your mind, even after you have checked your answers and supposedly reaffirmed your understanding.

So here's what you should do:

- **Do not attempt a multiple-choice question until you know that you have a strong understanding of the relevant material**
The first multiple-choice questions that you come across on any given topic might in fact be on the test you do in class on that topic. So you need to be really sure that you understand the material fully before you take the test – and you can do this by reviewing the material thoroughly, and, if possible, by finding an opportunity to explain it to a friend. You will find that putting the ideas into words greatly increases the robustness of your understanding – and no doubt you'll help the friend, too.

- **Stop before you look at the possible answers**
This applies to all multiple-choice questions you do, including those on the exam itself. Once you have read the question (not the possible answers), *mentally pause*. Reaffirm your own understanding and decide what you believe the answer to be, *before you look at the answers*. You might just have to glance at the answers to get an idea of the *kind* of thing that is being asked for, but make sure throughout the process that *your* thinking is dominant – your *correct* thinking, as opposed to the bogus thinking of the incorrect answers.

You will find in the pages that follow many multiple-choice questions, all of the style and level that you are likely to encounter on the AP Statistics exam. Some of them are straightforward, and some possibly challenging. You can use them all for practice of the steps given here, and to re-affirm the strong understanding of statistics that you have built up during the course. Do well!

Guidance for the Free-Response Section

Since the exam was first given in 1997, the readers have seen, over and over again, particular mistakes that students make in their approach and in their answering of the questions. Here's how to avoid those mistakes:

- **Use your time wisely**
As mentioned above, Question 6 will count for 25% of your free-response grade, so it's important that you restrict yourself to 13 minutes for each of Questions 1-5, thereby leaving yourself with the 25 minutes that you need for Question 6. Some teachers tell their students to start with Question 1, then do Question 6, and then complete the remaining questions.

- **Write answers that are clear, succinct, and complete**

Read the question carefully, decide what you need to say, and say just that. If you write long rambling answers, you are probably wasting valuable time and you are in danger of writing something incorrect and therefore losing credit. (And don't feel that you have to fill the space provided for your answer.)

- **Always answer in the context of the question**

For example, if the question is about plants and fertilizer, your answers must refer to plants and fertilizer.

- **Always show your work**

Some students find this hard to believe, but in AP Statistics, a numerical answer with no work shown, or a written statement with no explanation, will receive *no credit*.

- **Give just one answer to the question**

If you give two or more solutions or explanations, then you will be graded on the least correct of your answers. So it's up to you to decide which answer to submit. Cross out the other solution with a pencil – you can always erase your crossing out if you change your mind later.

- **Include all the steps of your argument**

For example, one question described a phone survey that is designed to estimate the proportion of an adult population that does not have a high school diploma. Students were asked to state one form of bias and to describe its effect on the result of the survey. Many students pointed out that phone surveys ignore people who have no phone, and people without phones will often not have high school diplomas. But the students failed to go on to say that this would result in an *underestimate* of the proportion of the population who do not have a high school diploma. It may seem obvious, but you have to say it.

- **When making a comparison, be sure to include consideration of both of the items that are being compared**

Suppose, for example, you are explaining that in a particular situation a Type II error is more serious than a Type I error. Then it's important that you describe the seriousness of a Type II error *and* explain why a Type I error is *less* serious.

- **Naming is not enough for description**

For example, if you are asked to describe a bias involved in a survey, and your response is "response bias," then you have only *named* the bias, not *described* it. Credit would only be given to students who explain what is happening and what effect it might have on the survey.

- **Interpreting the value includes <u>giving</u> the value**

Let's say you are given a computer display and you are asked to interpret the value of the correlation, r. Then you need to include the *value* of r in your answer.

- **When drawing a graph, make sure that you include labels and scales**
Label every axis and scale every axis. And, very importantly, if you're using a comparative display, such as a back-to-back stemplot or parallel boxplots, then make sure that you show which part of the diagram refers to which of the groups that are being compared.

- **If you can't do one part of a question, don't assume that you will be unable to do the rest of the question.**

- **If you need the answer to an earlier part of the question, and you were unable to do that part, make up a feasible answer**
An incorrect answer to, for example, part (a), correctly used in part (b), will gain full credit for part (b). So if you couldn't do part (a), make up a feasible answer and use it in part (b).

- **Be prepared for Question 6 to involve ideas that you haven't covered in class**
This is the idea of Question 6 – to have you think for yourself in a new situation. So keep calm, and set about doing what the question asks you to do – you have been thinking statistically for almost a year, and so the ideas are very unlikely to be beyond you.

General Guidance

- **Know the material**
This is possibly stating the obvious, but there's no replacement for a full knowledge and understanding of the material that has been covered in the course. Be aware, in particular, that the multiple-choice questions can test you on any detail that you have encountered.

- **Retain your intelligence!**
A question might at first seem to be different from anything that you have encountered during the year, but if you have paid attention during the course there will be very little in the exam that is truly beyond your understanding. And everything in statistics is logical – so if you retain your common sense and explain your thoughts, you will probably get the question right. (A few good nights' sleep before the exam will help with this!)

PART II: THE TOPICS

1. Graphical and Numerical Methods for Describing Data

You will need to be able to construct the following types of displays and draw conclusions from them:

☐ bar chart
☐ dotplot
☐ stemplot
☐ boxplot
☐ histogram

You will need to be able to draw conclusions from a

☐ cumulative (relative) frequency curve

For a given set of data, you should be able calculate and draw conclusions from the

☐ median
☐ quartiles
☐ percentiles
☐ interquartile range
☐ range
☐ mean
☐ variance
☐ standard deviation
☐ … and all of the above when the data are given in the form of a frequency distribution

You should also be able to:

☐ describe shapes of distributions, including positive and negative (right and left) skewness
☐ decide by doing calculations which value(s) is/are outliers
☐ comment on the appropriateness of the use of measures such as the mean and the standard deviation for particular sets of data
☐ know the effect of positive (or negative) skewness on the relationship between the mean and the median
☐ calculate the new values of measures such as the mean, median, standard deviation, etc., after the original dataset has been transformed by addition/subtraction and/or multiplication/division
☐ calculate z-scores and use them to compare the positions of particular scores within their respective distributions

Top Tips

- **Know how to describe shapes of distributions**

If you believe that a distribution is roughly symmetrical, then that is exactly the phrase to use: "roughly symmetrical." Never say "normal," as we can never be that precise, and do not say "evenly distributed," as that could be taken to mean something else. In some circumstances, "approximately normal" is accepted, but even this is dangerous, since in the case of boxplots it is not possible to say that a distribution that is roughly symmetrical will in fact be shaped like a normal distribution. So "roughly symmetrical" is the phrase to use!

- **Know how to compare distributions**

Having been given a comparative display, such as a back-to-back stemplot or parallel boxplots, you are very often asked to compare the distributions. In this situation you are expected to make your comparison in terms of <u>center</u>, <u>spread</u>, and <u>shape</u>, and you have to use phrases that actually compare – such as "is greater than" or "is less than." Saying, for example, "The median for the boys is 71 inches while the median for the girls is 66.5 inches" is not enough, since you haven't pointed out that 71 is bigger than 66.5. Here's a model answer from a student who has been asked to compare a set of boys' heights to a set of girls' heights:

> The center of the distribution for the boys (around 71 inches) is greater than the center of the distribution for the girls (around 67 inches).
>
> The range for the boys (8 inches) is greater than the range for the girls (6 inches).
>
> The distribution of the boys' heights is positively skewed. The distribution of the girls' heights is roughly symmetrical.

Notice that you are not required to use actual measures, such as medians, but if you choose to use them, and do so correctly, that will be accepted.

- **In graphs, make sure that you use proper labeling**

As mentioned in the guidance for the free-response section, when you draw a graph, make sure that your axes are scaled and labeled. And, very importantly, when you are drawing a comparative display such as a back-to-back stemplot or parallel boxplots, be sure to label which part of the diagram refers to which of the groups that are being compared.

- **Use the phrase "Middle 50%"**

If you are looking at a boxplot of, for example, girls' heights, and you want to refer to the box in the middle of the graph, the phrase to use is "the middle 50% of the girls' heights." Remember that the *interquartile range* is something else – it's the result you get when you subtract the lower (first) quartile from the upper (third) quartile.

- **Know how to interpret the standard deviation**

Let's suppose you know that the standard deviation of the girls' heights is 2.83 inches, and you are asked to interpret this value. Here's a model answer:

> 2.83 inches is a typical deviation of a girl's height from the mean height of the girls.

Notice that our model student gives the answer in context!

- **Only use the empirical rule in the case of a normal distribution**

The empirical rule states that in a normal distribution, approximately 68% of the observations fall within one standard deviation of the mean, approximately 95% of the observations fall within two standard deviations of the mean, and approximately 99.7% of the observations fall within three standard deviations of the mean. Many students make the mistake of using the empirical rule when it is not known that the distribution is normal. So keep away from the empirical rule unless you are certain that you are dealing with a quantity that is normally distributed, and even then it is advisable to preface your remarks by saying, "We know that the distribution is approximately normal, and so…"

- **Remember that there is no merit in skewness**

Suppose we know that the distribution of salaries paid by a company is positively skewed. This means that the spread of the salaries above the center of the distribution is greater than the spread of the salaries below the center of the distribution. It doesn't tell us anything about whether this company is paying high salaries or low salaries.

2. Correlation and Regression

Correlation, and Linear Regression

You should be able to:

☐ draw a scatterplot

☐ use a scatterplot to describe the closeness to a linear relationship

☐ use a scatterplot to describe the direction of a relationship (positive or negative)

☐ determine the value of the correlation, r, and the equation of the least squares regression line from computer output

☐ interpret the value of the correlation

☐ interpret the slope of the regression line

☐ decide whether the y-intercept of the regression line has a meaningful interpretation and, if so, give this interpretation

☐ use the regression line to estimate a value

☐ explain the inappropriateness of extrapolation

☐ explain that the value of the correlation is unaffected by adding a constant to all of the x-values (or y-values) and by multiplying all the x-values (or y-values) by a constant

☐ interpret the value of r^2

☐ calculate residuals or use residuals to calculate actual values

☐ draw a residual plot

☐ use a residual plot to establish the appropriateness (or not) of a linear model

Nonlinear Regression

You should:

☐ understand that transforming the variables can produce a linear fit

☐ be able to determine the appropriateness of a linear model using a residual plot

☐ be able to translate the linear fit of the transformed variables into the nonlinear fit of the original variables

☐ know that a linear fit for $\log y$ against x implies an exponential relationship between y and x, and a linear fit for $\log y$ against $\log x$ implies a power relationship between y and x.

 Top Tips

• **Know how to interpret the correlation, r**
For this you are expected to address the *strength*, *direction*, and *linearity* of the relationship, *in context*. So here's a model answer:

> $r = 0.769$. There is a moderately strong, positive, linear relationship between the height of the plant and the amount of fertilizer used.

Students in class often ask how large r needs to be in order for the relationship to be classified as "strong," "moderately strong," or "weak." This is not straightforward to answer as it depends on the size of the sample and, to some extent, the context. Consequently, the readers of the exam are relatively lenient on this point. Just make a decision, and your answer will probably be accepted.

• **Know how to interpret the slope of the regression line**
Let's suppose that the regression line relating running speed in mph (x) and pulse rate in beats per minute (y) has equation $\hat{y} = 62.143 + 15.953x$, and you are asked to interpret the slope of the regression line. Here's a model answer:

> For each one mile per hour increase in running speed, the <u>predicted</u> pulse rate increases by 15.953 beats per minute.

The word "predicted" could be replaced by "expected," or you could say that the pulse rate increases by "approximately" 15.953 beats per minute. Whatever your choice, you have to include a word that indicates that it's not the *actual* pulse rates that increase according to the given equation.

Likewise, if you were interpreting the y-intercept, you would need to say that it is the *predicted* pulse rate when the running speed is zero.

- **When giving the equation of the regression line, define x and $\hat{y}$**

Let's suppose that you've been given a computer display that includes the slope and the y-intercept in the example above, and that you've been asked to state the equation of the regression line. Then it is not enough just to say "$\hat{y} = 62.143 + 15.953x$." You have to state that x is the running speed and $\hat{y}$ is the predicted pulse rate.

Alternatively, you can state the equation in words:
Predicted pulse rate = 62.143 + 15.953 (speed).

- **Know and understand the interpretation of r^2**

Let's suppose that a boy's running speed is calculated on each of his birthdays. A scatterplot is constructed, plotting speed against age, and the value of r^2 is found to be 0.751. Here's a model interpretation of this value of r^2:

> 75.1% of the variation in running speed is explained by the least-squares regression line relating speed and age.

Many students decide that this is very complicated, and resort to memorizing the interpretation (with varying degrees of success). However, the concepts involved are not really all that complex, so we will spend a short time now getting to grips with the relevant ideas.

So let's return to the example of the boy and his running speed, and let's assume that his running speed has a precise linear relationship with his age. The scatterplot will look like this:

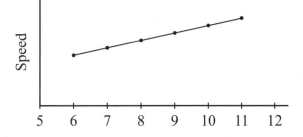

The boy's running speeds are not all the same, so there is some variation in running speed. All of this variation in running speed is explained by the fact that the boy is getting older and that his speed is related to his age by the straight line.

But, even if basically the boy's speed is linearly related to his age, there will be variations *from* the line due to various factors on his birthdays (what he has eaten, how tired he is, etc.). So the scatterplot is more likely to look like this:

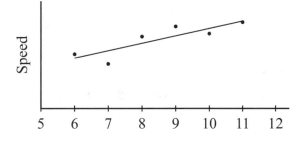

Given that the line has remained unchanged, there will now be *more* variation in the boy's speeds. (Either this makes intuitive sense to you, or you will have to accept this fact.) Some of that variation is explained by the fact that the boy is getting older and that his speed is related to his age by the straight line, and the rest is explained by the fact that the points are not exactly on the line. The proportion of the variability in speed that *is* explained by the straight line relationship is r^2.

3. Observational Studies and Experiments

You will need to:

☐ know what distinguishes an experiment from an observational study

Observational Studies

You will need to:

☐ understand why causation cannot be inferred from an observational study
☐ know what is meant by a census, and when it would be used
☐ know the definition of a simple random sample (SRS) and know how an SRS would be obtained

You should know how the following sampling methods would be implemented and why they would be used:

☐ stratified random sampling
☐ cluster sampling
☐ convenience sampling

You should be aware of the need to avoid, and be able to delineate the effect of, the forms of bias known as:

☐ undercoverage (selection) bias
☐ nonresponse bias
☐ response bias

Experimental design

You should know and understand the vocabulary of

☐ explanatory variables (factors) and response variables, levels of explanatory variables, and treatments

You should know:

☐ how and why to randomize the assignment of experimental subjects to the groups

- □ why there is need for a control group
- □ how and why to use a placebo
- □ single blinding: what it is, when it is possible, why it is used, and how it is achieved
- □ double blinding: what it is, when it is possible, why it is used, and how it is achieved
- □ blocking: why block, according to what variable, and how
- □ how to make a matched pairs design, and why this is advantageous
- □ the meaning of replication, and why it is needed
- □ to what extent the result of an experiment can be generalized to the whole population

Top Tips

• Confounding variables

Suppose that an observational study has revealed that people who exercise regularly tend to have lower blood pressure than people who do not, and you are asked to explain, giving an example of a possible confounding variable, why this does not mean that regular exercise <u>causes</u> low blood pressure. Here's a model answer:

> It may well be that people who exercise regularly tend to eat healthy food, and people who do not exercise regularly tend not to eat healthy food. In which case, it could be the healthy food that is causing the low blood pressure, not the exercise.

The link between exercise and healthy food, provided here by the phrase "tend to be the sort of people who…" is all-important. Students who say, "There are other factors, such as healthy food, that promote low blood pressure" are not addressing this link, and are therefore not explaining how the study could have turned out in the way that it did without regular exercise causing low blood pressure.

• Remember that sample size is rarely the problem

If you are asked to describe a problem in the design of an observational study, the sample size being too small is very unlikely to be the correct answer. The reason for this is that the mathematics that would be used to analyze the result would take account of the sample size. More likely, you should be looking for a source of *bias* (see the next tip).

• Know how to describe bias

Let's suppose that you are given the design of an observational study and you are asked to describe some form of bias that might be involved. You will need to explain that the issue you delineate is likely to make the result of the study inaccurate in *one direction*, and you should state *which* direction (up or down) it is likely to push the result.

For example, suppose a student wishes to estimate the mean amount of sleep for students at her school. She asks every fifth student entering the school, up to the time that the school day starts. The fact that she misses the students who are late to school is a source of bias since those who are late are likely to have had less sleep on average, and so the survey is likely to *over*estimate the mean amount of sleep. Without the likely effect on the survey, you have not described why this undercoverage is a source of bias.

- **Don't talk about sampling in the context of experiments**

Experiments are usually done with volunteers (if the experimental units are people) and very rarely with a random sample from the population being considered. What happens in experiments is *random assignment* to the groups.

- **Know how to describe the need for a control group**

Let's suppose that an experiment to test the effectiveness of a new drug for reducing blood pressure is being described, and you are asked to explain why a control group is needed. Here's a model answer:

> If you didn't have a control group and the subjects' blood pressures were on average significantly reduced, then you wouldn't know whether this reduction had come about as a result of the drug or as a result of some external factor such as an increase in sunshine. If, however, you have a group that is <u>not</u> given the drug, and this group does <u>not</u> on average experience a decrease in blood pressure, then we might be able to conclude that the drug is effective.

Two things about this external factor: First, it should not be referred to as a confounding variable, as it will affect *all* of the subjects – in other words there isn't a link with *one* of the groups. Second, it should be something that could feasibly affect all the subjects – it's no good saying, for example, that the subjects might be getting more sleep, unless you think there's something in the design of the experiment that will encourage all of the subjects to get more sleep.

- **Be very careful how you use the phrase "confounding variable"**

Think back to the first tip in this section, and note once more that for a variable to be a confounding variable, its values must differ systematically between the groups in the study. The eating of healthy food (or not) was acceptable as a confounding variable because it was suggested that those who exercise tend to eat healthy food and those who do *not* exercise tend *not* to eat healthy food. When you're answering a question, unless you're absolutely sure that the variable you're talking about differs between the groups in the study, it's best to avoid saying "confounding variable," and use, instead, a phrase such as "another variable that might affect the subjects' blood pressures" (or whatever the response variable happens to be).

- **Know how to achieve random assignment**

For example, suppose the question concerns an experiment that uses 50 volunteers, and you have to describe how to randomly assign them to two groups of 25 – a treatment group and a control group. Here's a model solution:

> Put the names of the 50 volunteers on pieces of paper and put the pieces of paper in a hat. Mix the pieces of paper, and then pick names from the hat at random. The first 25 names picked will go into the treatment group, and the remaining people will go into the control group.

This "hat method" will always work, so it's a good idea to use this approach, unless some other method is specified. There are two things to be careful about with this method. First, make sure that you include the instruction to mix the names and/or to pick them at random from the hat. Second, be sure to specify *which* group the first 25 (or whatever) names go into. Just saying "one of the groups" is not enough.

There's another method that students often use which does *not* constitute complete randomization: "Take a list of the volunteers and flip a coin for each volunteer. If the coin comes up heads, the volunteer goes into the treatment group, and if it's tails the volunteer goes into the control group. Once you have a group of 25, put the remaining volunteers into the other group." This doesn't constitute complete randomization as, for example, the last two people on the list are very likely to end up in the same group.

- **If you are asked for a "completely randomized design," this means that you should not include blocking**

- **Be careful not to say that randomization or blocking will "eliminate" differences between the groups**

Randomization (random assignment) ensures that any differences between the groups occur through bad luck only. It doesn't *eliminate* differences between the groups.

Blocking, by age for example, will ensure that the groups are *very similar* in terms of age, but it will not *eliminate* age differences between the groups.

- **Give complete answers to questions about blinding**

Let's suppose that a question cites an experiment to evaluate a treatment for clothing fabric, the treatment being designed to help people who suffer from skin inflammation. You are told in the stem of the question that the treatment leaves the fabric unchanged in appearance, and you are asked in one part of the question to state whether the experiment could be conducted in a double blind manner.

Now "double blind" means first that the participants do not know whether they are being given the treated or the untreated material, and second that the people who measure the response variable (the effect of the material on the skin) do not know who received the treated or the untreated material.

For the first criterion, it is necessary that you state in your answer that *we are told that the treatment leaves the fabric unchanged in appearance*, and so therefore that it is possible for the participants not to know which group they're in.

For the second criterion, be sure that you state that *the people who measure the effect of the fabric on the skin* do not know who received the treated or the untreated material. Just to say that the "experimenters" don't know is not enough.

- **Understand the rationale for – and the implementation of – blocking**

Let's suppose that an experiment is being designed to compare two treatments to prevent hair loss in men. We will look now at why and how blocking might be used in this context.

Why do we need blocking? Suppose that we believe that *older men will react less well than younger men* to these treatments. We therefore want our treatment groups to be as close as possible in terms of age, so that if we find a difference between the two groups in terms of their reactions to the treatments, we then know that this difference is unlikely to have anything to do with any age differences between the two groups. This is achieved by blocking by age.

Blocking is implemented as follows: First, the participants are split into *blocks* according to their age (for example, a block consisting of the two oldest men, a block consisting of the next two oldest men, and so on). Second the *treatments* are assigned randomly within each block (so, to continue the example, you flip a coin to find out which of the two oldest men gets treatment A and which gets treatment B, and so on for the other blocks). It is clear then that the two treatment groups (the group of subjects who are given treatment A and the group of subjects who are given treatment B) are very similar in terms of age.

It's important to remember that blocks consist of *similar* experimental units.

4. Probability and Simulation

You should understand and be proficient with the following:

- ☐ Venn diagrams and the "addition rule": $P(A \cup B) = P(A) + P(B) - P(A \cap B)$
- ☐ mutually exclusive events
- ☐ conditional probability
- ☐ probability and conditional probability from tables of frequencies
- ☐ independent events: are given events independent?
- ☐ use of $P(A \cap B) = P(A) \cdot P(B)$ for independent events
- ☐ use of tree diagrams
- ☐ reverse conditional probabilities (sometimes referred to as "Bayes' Rule")
- ☐ "without replacement" problems (e.g., when selecting four vehicles at random without replacement from a set of 10 sedans and 5 SUVs, what is the probability that they are all sedans?)
- ☐ use of a table of random digits to simulate probabilities such as 0.3, 5/9, 0.47

Top Tips

- **Understand mutually exclusive and independent events**

Keep the two ideas separate in your mind.

Two events are **mutually exclusive** if they can't both happen at the same time. For example, suppose we have a set of 40 cards consisting of 10 red cards (numbered 1–10), 10 blue cards (numbered 1–10), 10 green cards (numbered 1–10), and 10 purple cards (numbered 1–10). We will we pick one card at random. Let A be the event that the card is red and let B be the event that the card is green. Then the events A and B are mutually exclusive, since the card that we pick can't be both blue and green. Notice that if two events A and B are mutually exclusive, then $P(A \cap B) = 0$. The meaning of "mutually exclusive" is easy to remember because of the word "exclusive." The events *exclude* each other in the sense that if one of the events is happening, the other one can't be happening.

Two events are **independent** if they don't affect each other – that's what the word *independent* means. The easiest way to think of this is when we're doing two things that clearly have no effect on each other, such as flipping a coin and rolling a cube with faxes numbered 1 through 6. If A is that event that the coin shows a head and B is the event that the cube shows a six, then clearly the probability that B happens is unaffected by whether or not A has happened. To look at this another way, we're saying that $P(B \mid A)$ and $P(B)$ are the same.

But we need also to be aware of the possibility of independence when just *one* thing is happening. Let's return to the set of 40 cards mentioned above. Picking one card at rondom, let A be the event that the card is purple and let B be the event that the card is an 8. Then $P(B) = 4/40 = 1/10$ and $P(B \mid A) = 1/10$. Knowing that A is happening makes no difference to the probability that B is happening. So these two events A and B are independent also.

Suppose, on the other hand, that A is the event that the number on the card is greater than 7, and B is the event that the number on the card is an 8. Then $P(B) = 4/40 = 1/10$ and $P(B \mid A) = 4/12 = 1/3$. Knowing that A is happening changes the probability that B is happening. So, in this case, the events A and B are *not* independent.

Independence can be checked in many different ways. Any one of the statements, $P(B \mid A) = P(B)$, $P(A \mid B) = P(A)$, and $P(A \mid B) = P(A \mid B^c)$, is sufficient to prove independence, as is any statement that demonstrates that one event happening or not happening does not affect the probability that the other is happening. The statement that $P(A \cap B) = P(A) \cdot P(B)$ is also sufficient for proving that the events A and B are independent.

- **Understand the relationship between mutually exclusive and independent events**

Having told you to keep the two ideas separate in your mind (which you should definitely do until you are confident with them), we are now going to relate the two.

If two events are mutually exclusive, then knowing that one of them is happening means that the other *can't* be happening. So the events very much do affect each other, meaning that they are *not* independent.

Now looking at this relationship the other way around, if two events A and B are independent, then $P(A \cap B) = P(A) \cdot P(B)$, and so, unless one of $P(A)$ or $P(B)$ is zero, $P(A \cap B)$ can't be zero, and so A and B are not mutually exclusive.

- **When you are asked to describe a simulation process, be sure to give all the steps**
You need to include: where in the random digit table you will start, in what direction you will move, how many digits at a time you will use, what sets of digits are assigned to what outcome (including, possibly, some to be ignored), to ignore repeats (if applicable), what governs when the run of the simulation will stop, and what needs to be written down (e.g. the total score or the mean score) once the run of the simulation is finished.

- **When you are asked to carry out a simulation process, be sure to give the summary information that is required**
A question could ask you to perform five runs of your simulation, and to note the mean score for each run. Be sure that you actually carry out the second part of the instruction!

5. Random Variables

You should be familiar with the following:

- ☐ distinguishing between discrete and continuous random variables
- ☐ forming a probability distribution from given information
- ☐ representing a probability distribution in graph form
- ☐ finding the mean, variance, and standard deviation of a random variable from its probability distribution
- ☐ calculating probabilities from a probability density function using areas (for continuous random variables)
- ☐ recognizing that a random variable is binomially distributed, and calculating probabilities
- ☐ the formulas for the mean and standard deviation of a binomially distributed random variable
- ☐ recognizing that a random variable is geometrically distributed, and calculating probabilities
- ☐ problems using the normal distribution

You should also know the following:

- ☐ If $Y = aX + b$, where a and b are constants, then $E(Y) = aE(X) + b$ and $\mathrm{Var}(Y) = a^2\mathrm{Var}(X)$ (and so that $\sigma_Y = |a|\sigma_X$)
- ☐ $E(X + Y) = E(X) + E(Y)$ and, if X and Y are independent, that $\mathrm{Var}(X + Y) = \mathrm{Var}(X) + \mathrm{Var}(Y)$ (and consequently that $\sigma_{aX+bY} = \sqrt{a^2\sigma_X^2 + b^2\sigma_Y^2}$)
- ☐ $\mathrm{Var}(X - Y) = \mathrm{Var}(X) + \mathrm{Var}(Y)$
- ☐ If the random variables X and Y are independent and normally distributed, and a, b are constants (positive or negative), then $aX + bY$ is normally distributed. (Note that since b can be negative, this includes *subtraction* of multiples of independent normally distributed random variables.)

Top Tips

The fields of probability and random variables are the most numerical in the course, and so the free-response questions on these topics have often been the ones that are most successfully answered by students. The most common sources of error, apart from not knowing the material, tend to involve not showing adequate work – and this is what we will concern ourselves with in the tips for this section.

- **If you are asked to find the mean and/or the standard deviation (or variance) of a random variable using its probability distribution, use the formulas and write out the calculations**
It is possible to find the mean and the standard deviation of a discrete random variable using a calculator. However, if you use this method, it is very difficult to show your work in such a way that will get you full credit. The best approach, therefore, is to use the formulas and write out your calculations, and then you can always check your answers using the calculator if you have time.

- **Any time you use your calculator, show your work in some way that doesn't use calculator notation**
If, for example, you are dealing with the normal distribution, draw the normal curve and add to it the relevant information. If you are finding a probability derived from the binomial distribution, either show the formula with the numbers plugged in, or, if you are using one of the calculator functions, state in words or in mathematical notation (not calculator notation!) the fact that the relevant quantity is binomially distributed, the value of n, the value of p, and what it is you are finding the probability of. To generalize, you need to show, in mathematical notation or in words, all the quantities you use in your calculation.

- **In questions involving standard distributions such as binomial, geometric, and normal distributions, be sure to state the distribution and the parameters as well as providing a calculation**
For example, suppose that a question states that a cube with faces numbered 1 through 6 will be rolled 8 times, and asks for the probability that 3 or fewer sixes will result. The numerical answer to this question can be obtained directly with a calculator (using binomcdf(8,1/6,3), for example). However, in order to receive full credit you need to state that the distribution of the number of sixes is binomial and that the parameters are $n = 8$ and $p = 1/6$, as well providing a calculation of the numerical answer to the question.

6. Sampling Distributions

You should:

☐ know the language and notation of population parameters and sample statistics

☐ be able to compare two statistics according to their lack of bias and their low variability

☐ know that the sampling distribution of the sample mean, $\bar{x}$, has mean μ and standard deviation $\sigma/\sqrt{n}$, and is normal when the population is normally distributed

□ know that for a large sample size the sampling distribution of the sample mean is approximately normal (the Central Limit Theorem)

□ be able to solve problems involving the sampling distribution of the sample mean

□ be able to solve problems involving the sampling distribution of the sample proportion

□ know the nature of the *t*-distributions and how they relate to the standard normal distribution, $N(0,1)$

Top Tips

The field of sampling distributions forms a backbone to the whole study of statistics, and can at first seem very complicated. It is, in fact, quite easy to understand once you get clear in your mind what is really happening. So we concentrate here on helping you to get a full understanding of the ideas involved.

- **Understand the difference between population parameters and sample statistics**

Examples of population parameters are the population mean, μ, the population standard deviation, σ, and the population median (for which there is no standard notation). Examples of sample statistics are the sample mean, $\bar{x}$, the sample standard deviation, s, and the sample median. Sample statistics (sometimes called just "statistics") are used to estimate population parameters (sometimes called just "parameters"), and you should be aware that, for example, it might be suggested that you use the sample *median* to estimate the population *mean*.

Bear in mind that it is not always the population *mean* that is being estimated. For example, the sample standard deviation is designed to be an estimator for the population standard deviation.

- **Understand why the standard deviation of the sampling distribution of the sample mean is smaller than the population standard deviation**

Let's consider a very large population – all the women in a town, for example. Let the population mean height be μ.

Imagine picking a woman at random and measuring her height. Roughly how far might you expect this height to be from μ? You are estimating the population standard deviation, σ.

Now imagine picking a random sample of 20 women, and finding the sample mean height, $\bar{x}$. How far might you expect $\bar{x}$ to be from μ? The answer is a lot less than σ, since any extremely large heights in the sample are likely to be balanced out by extremely small heights in the sample.

So the standard deviation of $\bar{x}$ is less than the population standard deviation. The precise formula is that the standard deviation of $\bar{x}$ is $\sigma/\sqrt{n}$, where n is the size of the sample.

- **Understand that the Central Limit Theorem makes sense intuitively**

Imagine a very large company for which the salaries are not normally distributed but are, let's say, positively skewed. We will denote the mean salary for the company by μ.

Now imagine taking a large sample of, say, 50 salaries from this company, and finding the sample mean. We expect this sample mean to be very close to μ, since any extreme salary (in either direction) in the sample will be reduced in its impact by the majority of the other 49 salaries.

Now imagine taking many, many samples of size 50 and finding their sample means. We expect a great density of values around μ, with the density tailing off to each side of μ; looking like a normal distribution with mean μ, in fact.

Now, thinking about this carefully, you might want to argue that the distribution of the values of the sample means will be slightly positively skewed. This is in fact correct, but only very slightly, as, by the same argument as above, the effect on the sample mean of any extremely large values in the sample will be greatly reduced by the majority of other values in the sample.

You should be a little closer now to understanding why the Central Limit Theorem makes sense intuitively.

- **Understand where the t-distributions come from**

If we take a random sample of size n from a normally distributed population, then $(\bar{x} - \mu)/(\sigma/\sqrt{n})$ is normally distributed with mean 0 and standard deviation 1. If we replace the population standard deviation σ with the sample standard deviation s, we get $(\bar{x} - \mu)/(s/\sqrt{n})$, which is t-distributed with $n - 1$ degrees of freedom.

Now, the variability in $(\bar{x} - \mu)/(\sigma/\sqrt{n})$ is provided solely by $\bar{x}$, since everything else in the expression is a constant. However, when we replace the constant σ with s, we introduce more variability, since s, the sample standard deviation, has its own variability. This explains why the t-distributions have more variability than the standard normal distribution, $N(0,1)$.

Further, we can see that the larger the value of n, the less variability is attached to s, since for larger samples the sample standard deviation is a more accurate estimator of σ. So, as the number of degrees of freedom increases, the variance of the t-distribution decreases, getting closer and closer to the variance of the standard normal distribution, which is 1.

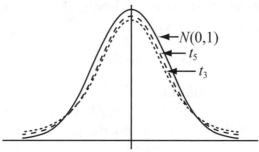

7. Confidence Intervals for Means and Proportions

You should know how to find the following intervals:

- z-interval for the population mean
- t-interval for the population mean
- z-interval for the population proportion
- z-interval for the difference between two population means
- two-sample t-interval for the difference between two population means
- paired t-interval for the difference between two population means
- z-interval for the difference between two population proportions

Additionally, you should know how to:

☐ interpret a confidence interval

☐ interpret a confidence level

☐ find the minimum sample size for a given margin of error

Top Tips

• **When asked to construct a confidence interval, perform all three steps**

This is very important. Any time you are asked for a confidence interval, you need to do the following:

1. Name the type of interval and check the conditions

   So you will need to say, for example, "This is a *t*-interval for the population mean," and then check the conditions for that type of interval. We will look at the details of how you should check the conditions in the next tip.

2. Mechanics

   This is the numerical work needed to calculate the interval. You should provide the formula, the formula with the numbers plugged in, and the result.

3. Interpretation of the interval

   For example, if the question asks you to find a 95% confidence interval for the mean height of all the women in a town, a model answer is as follows:

   > We are 95% confident that the mean height of all the women in the town is between 62.827 and 63.611 inches.

   Never use the words "probability" or "chance" when interpreting a confidence interval.

• **Do a complete check of the conditions**

You will first need to make a statement that we are told (or we have to assume) something about the randomness of the sample(s). In one-sample intervals we need one random sample. In two-sample intervals we need either two independent random samples, or random assignment of a set of objects to two groups (as in experiments). In a paired *t*-interval we need to know that the sample differences can be viewed as a random sample from a population of differences.

Then you will need to check the conditions for the type of interval you're calculating. There are three possibilities:

I. *z*- or *t*-intervals for population means where the sample size(s) is/are greater than 30

   In this case we are using the Central Limit Theorem, and you just need to state the sample size and note that it is greater than 30 (for a one-sample interval), or (for a two-sample interval) state both sample sizes and note that they are both greater than 30.

II. *z*- or *t*-intervals for population means where the sample size(s) is/are *not* greater than 30

Here, since we can't use the Central Limit Theorem, we are depending on the fact that the population(s) is/are normally distributed. Most likely, you will *not* be told that the population is normally distributed and you will be given the sample values. You have to justify the assumption that the population is normally distributed *by showing that the set of sample values roughly follows the pattern of a normal distribution*. This is done by drawing a graph (or pair of graphs for two-sample intervals) into your answer. If you draw a histogram or a boxplot you need to say that the distribution is roughly symmetrical and there are no outliers. If you draw a normal probability plot, you need to say that the pattern in the plot is roughly linear.

(Do not be overly concerned if your graph really doesn't look all that symmetrical (or linear, in the case of a normal probability plot). Remember that we're probably dealing with a small sample, and so some departure from symmetry in the sample values can be expected even if we're dealing with what is in fact a truly normally distributed population. If you're not certain, you should use a phrase such as "proceed with caution.")

III. z-intervals for population proportions

In this case you need to check (for a one-sample interval) that $n\hat{p} \geq 10$ and $n(1 - \hat{p}) \geq 10$, or (for a two-sample interval) that $n_1\hat{p}_1 \geq 10$, $n_1(1 - \hat{p}_1) \geq 10$, $n_2\hat{p}_2 \geq 10$, $n_2(1 - \hat{p}_2) \geq 10$. You need to write out the calculations for these checks – it's not enough just to say, for example, "$n\hat{p} \geq 10$ ✔, $n\hat{q} \geq 10$ ✔." (If your textbook gives a slightly different set of criteria, then it's fine to do whatever the book suggests. This applies to the numerical check in I. above, also.)

Failing to check the conditions completely when asked for a confidence interval is one of the most common mistakes on the exam, and will result in your getting at most half-credit for the confidence interval. So make absolutely sure that you do all that is required.

- **Know how to interpret the confidence <u>level</u>**

Not to be confused with interpretation of the confidence *interval*, which is Step 3 of the standard confidence interval answer, this is how to respond when you are asked, "What is the meaning of 95% confidence in this context?" Here's a model answer:

> 🖉 In 95% of samples, the resulting confidence interval will contain the true mean height of all the women in the town.

Let's explain this in slightly greater detail. At this stage we have generally calculated the confidence interval on the basis of one sample. We are now imagining taking a very large number of samples and, for each sample, calculating the confidence interval in the same way. Each sample will be different, and therefore all the confidence intervals will be different. The statement is that 95% of the confidence intervals will contain the true mean height of the women.

Notice that the only numbers contained in the model answer are "95." If you include any other numbers, then you're getting something wrong!

8. Hypothesis Tests for Means and Proportions

You will need to know the following hypothesis tests:

- z-test for the population mean
- t-test for the population mean
- z-test for the population proportion
- z-test for the difference between two population means
- two-sample t-test for the difference between two population means
- paired t-test for the difference between two population means
- z-test for the difference between two population proportions

Additionally, you should know how to:

- distinguish between one- and two-tailed tests
- interpret the p-value
  use critical values
- use a confidence interval to make a conclusion to a hypothesis test

Top Tips

- **When performing a hypothesis test, complete all four steps**
These are the four steps:

1. State the hypotheses

    You might say, for example:

    $H_0 : \mu = 63.5$

    $H_a : \mu > 63.5$

    It is good practice to define the parameter(s) you use. For the above example you might start by saying, "Let μ be the mean height of all the women in the town." However, if you use standard notation (μ for a population mean and p or π for a population proportion), you will get full credit for your hypotheses even if you don't define the parameter(s).

    In two-sample tests, use subscripts that refer specifically to the populations under consideration. For example, if a comparison is being made of a population of girls to a population of boys, use μ_G and μ_B rather than μ_1 and μ_2.

    You may, if you prefer, give the hypotheses in words rather than symbols, but be sure to make it clear that the hypotheses refer to *population* parameters.

2. Name the test, and check the conditions

    So you need to say, for example, "This is a t-test for the population mean," and go on to check the conditions. We'll give details about how to check the conditions in the next tip.

3. <u>Mechanics</u>

First, evaluate the test statistic, showing the formula and how you plug in the numbers. Then evaluate the *p*-value. (Alternative methods using critical values are accepted, but be aware that an understanding of *p*-values *and* critical values is required in the exam.) Also, be sure to state the number of degrees of freedom where applicable.

4. <u>Conclusion</u>

Here's a model conclusion:

> 🖉 Since the *p*-value is 0.021, which is less than 0.05, we reject H_0. We have sufficient evidence to conclude that the mean height of all the women in the town is greater than 63.5 inches.

Note that you do not *have* to use phrases such as "Reject / fail to reject H_0," in fact a phrase of this sort, without a conclusion in context such as the model answer above, would not be considered a complete conclusion. The conclusion must contain some reference to the size of the *p*-value ("less/greater than 0.05" or "which is small / not small"), and must be given in the context of the question. Be sure also to include the word "mean(s)" or "proportion(s)."

If your teacher has given you a different set of steps then that's fine, so long as you cover all of the above criteria.

- **Do a complete check of the conditions**

The conditions that need to be checked for hypothesis tests are almost identical to those for their equivalent confidence intervals (the exception is with the test/interval for a single proportion, where you use $n\hat{p} \geq 10$ and $n(1 - \hat{p}) \geq 10$ for the confidence interval and $np \geq 10$ and $n(1 - p) \geq 10$ for the hypothesis test). Nonetheless, we will look again at all the details here, since failure to correctly check the conditions for a hypothesis test is possibly the most common error in the exam.

You will first need to make a statement that we are told (or we have to assume) something about the randomness of the sample(s). In one-sample tests we need one random sample. In two-sample tests we need either two independent random samples, or random assignment of a set of objects to two groups (as in experiments). In a paired *t*-interval we need to know that the sample differences can be viewed as a random sample from a population of differences.

Then you will need to check the conditions for the type of test you're calculating. There are three possibilities:

I. *z*- or *t*-tests for population means where the sample size(s) is/are greater than 30

In this case we are using the Central Limit Theorem, and you just need to state the sample size and note that it is greater than 30 (for a one-sample test), or (for a two-sample test) state both sample sizes and note that they are both greater than 30.

II. *z*- or *t*-tests for population means where the sample size(s) is/are *not* greater than 30

Here, since we can't use the Central Limit Theorem, we are depending on the fact that the population(s) is/are normally distributed. Most likely, you will *not* be told that the population is normally distributed and you will be given the sample values. You have to justify the assumption that the population is normally distributed *by showing that the set of sample values roughly follows the pattern of a normal distribution*. This is done by drawing a graph (or pair of graphs for two-sample tests) into your answer. If you draw a histogram or a boxplot you need to say that the distribution is roughly symmetrical and there are no outliers. If you draw a normal probability plot, you need to say that the pattern in the plot is roughly linear.

(Do not be overly concerned if your graph really doesn't look all that symmetrical (or linear, in the case of the normal probability plot). Remember that we're probably dealing with a small sample, and so some departure from symmetry in the sample values can be expected even if we're dealing with what is in fact a truly normally distributed population. If you're not certain, you should use a phrase such as "proceed with caution.")

III. z-tests for population proportions

In this case you need to check (for a one-sample test) that $np \geq 10$ and $n(1-p) \geq 10$, or (for a two-sample test) that $n_1\hat{p}_1 \geq 10$, $n_1(1-\hat{p}_1) \geq 10$, $n_2\hat{p}_2 \geq 10$, $n_2(1-\hat{p}_2) \geq 10$. You need to write out the calculations for these checks – it's not enough just to say, for example, " $np \geq 10$ ✓, $n(1-p) \geq 10$ ✓." (If your textbook gives a slightly different set of criteria, then it's fine to do whatever the book suggests. This applies to the numerical check in I. above, also.)

- **Never "Accept H_0"**
To accept H_0 in the example in the first tip would be to say that the mean height of all the women in the town is exactly 63.5 inches, to an infinite number of decimal places. This is obviously a very strong statement, and one that cannot be justified. We only ever *have* convincing evidence or *do not have* convincing evidence of whatever is stated in H_a (and remember to give everything in your conclusion in *words*, as demonstrated in Part 4 of the first tip).

- **Know how to distinguish between the two-sample t-test and the paired t-test**
This applies to confidence intervals, also. Particularly when the correct test is the paired version, students over the years have been very poor at making the correct choice.

We're talking here about comparing means. If you have two samples, then it's a two-sample t-test. If you have one sample, with two numbers for each element of the sample, then it's a paired t-test. It's also a paired t-test if the data come from an experiment where the set of experimental units has been split into blocks of size 2 (matched pairs).

- **Know how to check the conditions for the paired t-test**
In this hypothesis test you work out the differences for the sample values, and test whether the mean difference is significantly less than, greater than, or different from zero. In order to do this, you need to justify the assumption that the population of differences is normally distributed. This is done by drawing a boxplot, histogram, or normal probability plot for the sample *differences*, and commenting in the same way as in option II in the tip above on checking the conditions. (You also, of course, have to state that we know or we assume that the set of sample differences is a random sample from the population of differences.)

- **Know how to interpret the p-value**
This is actually what hypothesis testing is all about, so we'll spend a little time on it.

We use hypothesis testing intuitively every day of our lives. Consider the following example:

Let's suppose that my wife leaves work at 4 p.m. every day. She either drives straight home (the journey takes about 20 minutes) or she runs some errands (of varying lengths).

If it gets to 4:25 p.m. and she's not yet home, I think to myself, "Given that she drove straight home, it's still quite possible that she would not be home by now." So I do not have evidence that she's running errands.

If, however, it gets to 4:40 p.m. and she's still not home, I think to myself, "Given that she drove straight home it's very unlikely that she would not be home by now." So I have evidence that she's running errands.

The p-value in the context of this example is the probability, given that she drove straight home, that she would not be home by now. When it gets to as late as 4:40 p.m. this p-value is small, so I reject the null hypothesis that she drove straight home in favor of the alternative hypothesis that she is running errands.

If you understand this example (which I hope you do!), you understand hypothesis testing.

When you are asked to interpret the p-value, you have to state that its value (0.021, for example) is the probability, given that H_0 is true, that the test statistic would be as large (or small – or different from zero for a two-tailed test) as the one obtained. As always, this statement must be given in the context of the question. So here's a model interpretation, when the t-statistic is 2.180 and the p-value is 0.021:

> 0.021 is the probability, given that the mean height of all the women in the town is 63.5 inches, that you would get a value of t as large as 2.180.

Remember that the t-statistic measures essentially the distance of the sample mean from the supposed population mean. So a slightly less precise but acceptable interpretation would be to say, "0.021 is the probability, given that the mean height of all the women in the town is 63.5 inches, that you would get a sample mean as far above 63.5 as the one obtained in our sample."

- **Know precisely how to use a confidence interval to make a conclusion to a hypothesis test**
Let's assume that you have found, or have been given, a 95% confidence interval for the difference of two population means or proportions.

If zero is in the confidence interval, then we do not have convincing evidence of a difference in the population means (or proportions) at the 5% level.

If zero is *not* in the confidence interval, then we *do* have convincing evidence of a difference in the population means (or proportions) at the 5% level.

This is easy to understand, since, if zero is not in the confidence interval, then it is not feasible that the difference in the population parameters is zero, or, in other words, we have convincing evidence of a difference in the population parameters. Notice that the conclusion we're getting from the confidence interval is for a *two-tailed* test.

9. The Chi-Square Tests

You should know how to perform the following three chi-square tests:

☐ goodness of fit

☐ independence

☐ homogeneity

Top Tips

- **Know how to distinguish between the three tests**

In the goodness of fit test there is one categorical variable, whereas in the tests for independence and homogeneity there are two. So, for example, the information given in a question on goodness of fit could be:

Color of Car	White	Black	Silver	Red	Other
Number of Cars Observed	101	62	54	50	120

The information given in a question on independence or homogeneity could be as in the following table, where the numbers in the table are counts of people:

	Disagree	No Opinion	Agree
Male	78	33	49
Female	66	55	39

So, in the first example there is one variable (color of car), and in the second there are two variables (gender and opinion).

All that remains now, therefore, is to be able to tell the difference between the tests for independence and homogeneity. A question on independence is likely to say something like, "Is there any evidence of an association between gender and opinion?" A question on homogeneity is likely to say something like, "Is there any evidence that the three category proportions are different for the two populations (males and females)?" The wording can vary, but the hard and fast way to tell between the two tests is as follows: If the counts in the table resulted from *one* sample then it would be a test for independence. If the counts resulted from *two* samples – a random sample of males and a random sample of females – it would be a test for homogeneity. Tests for independence always involve a single sample; tests for homogeneity involve two or more samples.

Once you have decided which test to perform, you will need to make sure that you use the correct wording. We'll leave you to look back in your class notes or your textbook and to learn exactly what you have to say.

Notice that in chi-square tests the numbers given are counts. In tests for proportions you are given counts or sample proportions. If the numbers given are measurements (or scores), then the hypothesis tests available to us are the tests for means and the test for the slope of the regression line.

- **Complete all four steps of the hypothesis test**

The four steps for hypothesis tests given in the previous section apply to chi-square tests, also.

In Step 2, the conditions to check are that the observed counts result from one (or more than one) random sample, and that the expected counts (which you should give in your answer) are all greater than 5. (There are variations on this latter criterion – it's fine to use whatever your textbook says.)

Be careful to word your conclusion (Step 4) correctly. If you are failing to reject H_0, then a correct answer could involve a double negative – for example, "We do not have convincing evidence that the proportions of car colors are not the same as the published proportions." Whatever you do, don't "accept H_0"!

- **Know how to perform the numerical steps of the chi-square tests on your calculator**

The calculator can be a significant time-saving device in this area of the syllabus, particularly with the tests for independence and homogeneity, so it's worth making sure that you know how to use it to perform these tests.

For the goodness of fit test, be aware that different calculators deal with the test in different ways, so make sure that you are familiar with the way to do it on *your* calculator.

In the tests for independence and homogeneity, the calculator will find the expected frequencies and will calculate the test statistic and the *p*-value for you. Make sure you know to achieve this!

You should also be aware that a multiple-choice question could test your ability to perform certain steps – for example, finding expected frequencies or the *p*-value – *without* using the chi-square test function on the calculator. So be sure that you can do this, also.

10. Inference for the Slope of the Regression Line

You should know how to

- ☐ perform the hypothesis test and find the confidence interval for the slope of the regression line using computer output
- ☐ perform the hypothesis test (and possibly find the confidence interval) using raw data
- ☐ interpret the values of s and s_b

Top Tips

- **Know how to use computer output**

Let's use an example for this. Suppose that a large number of students in a college take algebra. One year, at the end of the first quarter, a random sample of 20 students is taken, and the students in the sample are given a surprise exam. A list is compiled containing the quarter averages and the exam scores for those 20 students, and a linear regression is run, with the following results:

```
                    Dependent variable: Exam
Predictor              Coef        SE Coef         T           P
Constant          46.063584(1)    20.19293       2.28      0.0349
Quarter           0.3063584(2)    0.236814(3)    1.29(4)   0.2121(5)

S = 4.7749(6)    R-sq = 8.51%    R-sq (adj) = 3.42%
```

There are six numbers in the table that we should be concerned with here, and we will look at their relevance now.

(1) 46.064 is the y-intercept for the least squares regression line; that is, the value of a in $\hat{y} = a + bx$.

(2) 0.306 is the slope of the least squares regression line; that is, the value of b in $\hat{y} = a + bx$.

(3) 0.237 is the standard error of the slope of the regression line, often denoted by s_b.

(4) 1.29 is the value of the t-statistic in the t-test for the slope of the regression line (with null hypothesis H_0: $\beta = 0$).

(5) 0.212 is the p-value in the t-test for the slope of the regression line. It is important to note that this p-value is for the *two-tailed* test.

(6) 4.775 is the standard error about the least squares regression line, usually denoted by s.

- **Understand the meanings of s and s_b**

The formula for s, the standard error about the regression line, is $s = \sqrt{\dfrac{\sum (y - \hat{y})^2}{n - 2}}$. This quantity is a measure of the amount by which the points in the scatterplot vary vertically from the least squares regression line. Now, if we replace $(n - 2)$ by $(n - 1)$ in the formula for s, we get $\sqrt{\dfrac{\sum (y - \hat{y})^2}{n - 1}}$, which is the standard deviation of the residuals. Therefore s, being very close to this quantity, can itself be referred to as the standard deviation of the residuals. So, if you were asked to interpret the value of s for the example in the previous tip, you could say:

4.775 is the standard deviation of the residuals for the students' exam scores.

The formula for s_b, as given on the formula sheet provided in the exam, is $s_b = \dfrac{\sqrt{\dfrac{\sum(y-\hat{y})^2}{n-2}}}{\sqrt{\sum(x-\bar{x})^2}}$, but you are unlikely to be expected to use this formula. In order to understand what s_b represents, we need to think in the following way: In the example in the previous tip, one sample of 20 students was taken, and the regression line was found. Imagine now taking a very large number of samples, and finding the slope of the regression line for each. The statistic s_b is an estimate of the standard deviation of this set of slopes of regression lines. So here's a model interpretation of s_b:

> 🖉 0.237 is an estimate of the standard deviation of the slopes of the regression lines relating exam score and quarter score over all possible samples of 20 students.

- **Know how to perform the hypothesis test and construct the confidence interval**

The first thing to remember is that you should complete all four steps of the hypothesis test as given in Section 8 or, for the confidence interval, all three steps as given in Section 7. We will look at how to check the conditions in the next tip.

If you're given computer output, then, for the hypothesis test, you can use the t-value and the p-value given. (We saw how to locate these values in the first tip of this section.) For the confidence interval, state the formula $b \pm t^* \cdot s_b$, and use the values of b and s_b given in the computer output, along with the value of t^* given in the table of t critical values provided with the exam. (Note that the number of degrees of freedom is $n-2$, where n is the sample size.)

If you are *not* given computer output, then you will need to use the raw data provided. For the hypothesis test, you can calculate the relevant quantities using the calculator function designed to do this test. Do not be concerned about including the formulas – these are very unlikely to be required.

The confidence interval, when you're not given computer output, is a little tricky to find, unless you have one of the calculators that has the inbuilt function to do this. For this reason, the confidence interval using raw data is unlikely to be required in the exam.

- **Know how to check the conditions**

These are what textbooks call the "conditions (or assumptions) for the regression model." The concepts behind these conditions are sometimes considered complex, but the process of checking them is relatively straightforward.

We use the residual plot. Just as when we're checking for the appropriateness of a linear model, we are looking for a "random pattern," and here we're looking for randomness in two senses.

First, we need to check that there is no obvious curve. (Be reasonably tolerant – it's very hard to find a residual plot that doesn't show *some* evidence of a curve.)

Second, we need to check that we do <u>not</u> have one of the two following patterns:

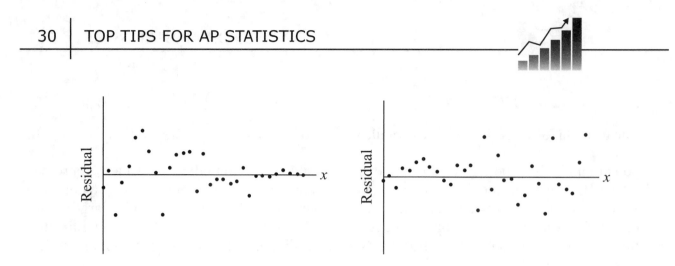

11. Errors in Hypothesis Testing

You should:

☐ know the meanings of Type I and Type II errors

☐ be able to describe Type I and Type II errors in a given context

☐ be able to compare the consequences of the two errors in a given context

☐ understand how the probabilities of Type I and Type II errors work

☐ know the meaning of *power*

✎ Top Tips

• **When comparing consequences, consider both types of error**
We already looked at this in the context of free-response questions in general, when talking about how to compare two things. Suppose that you are asked, in a particular scenario, which of the errors is more serious, and you believe that it is the Type II error. Then it's important that you not only describe why a Type II error could have serious consequences, but *also* describe why the consequences of a Type I error are not so serious.

• **Understand how the probabilities of Type I and II errors work**
Here's an easy way to think about this:

1. The probability of a Type I error is always the significance level of the test.

2. Therefore, you can reduce the probability of a Type I error by reducing the significance level. However, doing this will *increase* the probability of a Type II error, since reducing the significance level increases the probability that you will fail to reject H_0. When adjusting the significance level, if you gain with Type I errors then you lose with Type II errors, and vice versa.

3. The only way to decrease the probability of a Type II error without increasing the probability of a Type I error is to increase the sample size.

And there's one more thing you should be aware of:

The probability of a Type II error is different according to the true value of the population parameter being tested. Say, for example, that you are testing H_0: $\mu = 64.5$ against H_a: $\mu > 64.5$. If μ takes a value just above 64.5, such as 64.6, then H_a is true, but it's very unlikely that you will (correctly) reject H_0; in other words, there's a *high* probability of a Type II error. If, however, the true value of μ takes a value that is much larger than 64.5, such as 66.5, then it is very likely that you will (correctly) reject H_0; in other words, there's a *low* probability of a Type II error.

USING THE TI-NSPIRE ON THE AP STATISTICS EXAMINATION

By Heather Overstreet

This chapter will give you guidelines and tips for efficiently using the TI-Nspire calculator on the AP Statistics exam. The main focus is to provide condensed instructions for the functionality of the Nspire that you may use. First we will look at the four strands of the AP Statistics curriculum, and each of these strands has been broken into the specific topics that could arise on the exam. We will then look at the formula sheet that is provided on the AP exam, and the associated Nspire functions will be explained. Finally, we will look at the sort of multiple choice questions that might arise on the exam where the calculator is necessary or useful.

"BIG IDEAS" have also been included to provide important technology tips for the exam.

The TI-Nspire has had three different keypads: the Clickpad, the Touchpad, and the new CX. The Clickpad and Touchpad are interchangeable with the original handheld; however, the CX is the new Nspire with a slimmer design and a full color, backlit display. The instructions in this chapter use the CX keys; however, the key structure, as shown below, is exactly like the Touchpad with the exception of key shape.

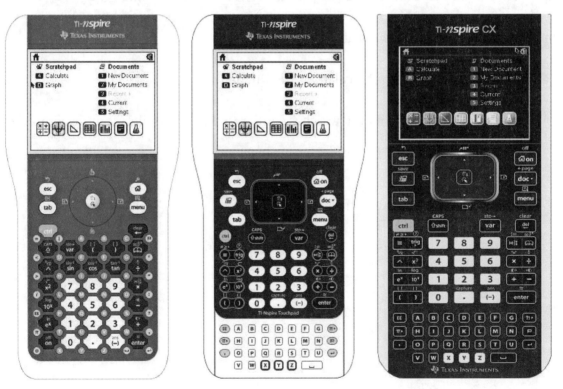

Instructions for the Clickpad will be given in parentheses if the keystrokes vary from the Touchpad or CX.

33

There are three main applications on the Nspire that are used in Statistics: *Lists & Spreadsheet*, *Data & Statistics*, and *Scratchpad* (or Calculator).

- In the Lists & Spreadsheet application, data sets can be entered into the columns. It is veryimportant that each column (data set) be given a name at the top of the column. The cell just below the heading is the formula cell. On the AP exam, you will probably not need this cell.

- Once a data set has been entered and named in the *Lists & Spreadsheet* page, a *Data & Statistics* page can graph it.

- The *Scratchpad* application is for quick calculations; this is the basic calculator screen. However, variables that are defined in a *Lists & Spreadsheet* page are not available in the *Scratchpad*. If the calculations require defined variables you will need to add a Calculator page.

Some Keystrokes that are Helpful to Remember

[ctrl] [esc] – undoes the last command. If you are computer savvy, you can also use [ctrl] [Z] which is the computer command to UNDO and [ctrl] [Y] to REDO the last command.

[ctrl] ◀ or ▶ - navigates between the pages or applications.

[⌨] ((⌂) (A)) - goes directly to the calculator Scratchpad

[ctrl] [menu] – accesses the shortcut menu, which is similar to the "right-click" on the computer mouse.

THE TOPIC AREAS

I. Exploring Data: What to do with a data set

BIG IDEA 1 Just because there is a data set, you do NOT necessarily need the calculator. READ and INTERPRET the problem before you start entering data into the calculator.

Here is a data set for the average number of hours of sleep per night for 20 AP Statistics students:

8	6.5	3	7	9	6.5	6	7	7.5	7
6	8	5	7.5	7	5.5	6	7	8	6

- Open a new document.

- Insert a Lists & Spreadsheet page: Press [ctrl] [I] and scroll down to Add Lists & Spreadsheet, and press [enter].

- Name column A: sleep and enter the data above.

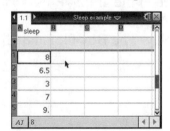

A. Summary Statistics

- In the Lists & Spreadsheet page, press [menu], Statistics, Stat Calculations, One-Variable Statistics.

- [tab] to [OK] and press [enter].

- Set up the next dialogue box as shown.

- Press [enter] and the summary statistics will be displayed.

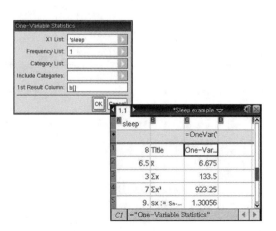

B. Graphical Displays: One data set

When graphing a data set, the Nspire does an excellent job of labeling the axes. If you are asked to display a graph on the exam, what you draw should match what you see on the screen. Always label and scale your axes!

- Insert a *Data & Statistics* page - [ctrl] [I] , arrow to *Add Data & Statistics* and press [enter].

- Press [tab] and *Click to Add Variable* on the horizontal axis will show the variables available. Select **sleep**.

    The data points will now move into a dotplot. This is the *default* display.

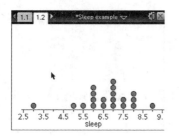

- To change the display, arrow up to an empty space in the graph. Press [ctrl] [menu] and you should see the options *Box Plot*, *Histogram*, *Normal Probability Plot*, and *Zoom*. Select each one to get the different graphical display. The Box Plot and Histograms are displayed below.

BOX PLOT

HISTOGRAM

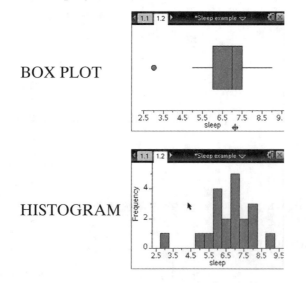

To change the width of the bars of the histogram press [ctrl] [menu] and select Bin Settings. You can change the Width and the Alignment to get a different display.

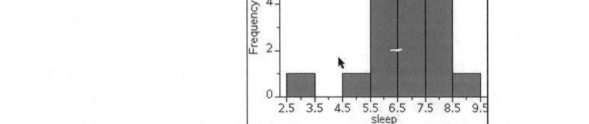

You may need to adjust the vertical axis if the bars extend beyond the top of the page. This can be done as follows.

o Using the touchpad, move the arrow to the vertical axis. You should see the arrow change to a double arrow.

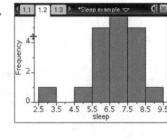

o When the double arrow appears, press and hold [image] until a closed hand appears ([image]).

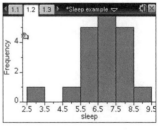

o Use the touchpad to adjust the axis. Press [image] when the tallest bar is completely visible and the hand will become the double arrow again.

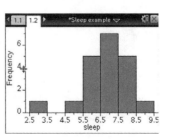

C. Graphical Displays: Comparing Data Sets

When you are asked to graph two univariate data sets, don't forget to LABEL both variables being displayed. Properly named lists in the Nspire will illustrate this idea.

Let's compare the number of hours of sleep between the AP Statistics students and a group of AP Calculus students. Below are the hours of sleep reported by 16 AP Calculus students.

9.6	5	5.5	5	7	5	6	7
6	6.5	6	6.5	6	5.5	7	6.5

- Insert another Lists & Spreadsheet page by pressing ⟨ctrl⟩ ⟨I⟩ and selecting Add Lists & Spreadsheet. Name column A: aps_sleep and press ⟨enter⟩. In the formula cell, press ⟨enter⟩ and select sleep. Name column B: apc_sleep and enter the 16 times.

- Insert a Data & Statistics page. Press ⟨tab⟩ and Click to Add Variable on the horizontal axis will show the variables available. Select aps_sleep.

- Arrow over the aps_sleep and press ⟨ctrl⟩ ⟨menu⟩. Arrow to Add X Variable, press ⟨enter⟩, and select apc_sleep. Both dotplots will now be displayed.

  The graphical displays can be changed using the instructions given in Section B, above.

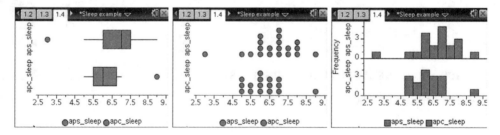

D. Bivariate Data

Students were asked how many hours per week they studied for a particular class during a grading period. The students' numerical grades are listed below along with the number of reported hours they studied each week.

Study Time	0.5	5	2	3	5	0	3	3.5	4
Grades	68	92	77	72	98	60	75	82	88

- Input the data into a new Lists & Spreadsheet page. Name column A: studytime and column B: grades.

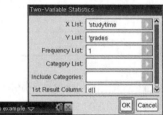

- Generate the summary statistics for variables: Press [menu], Statistics, Stat Calculations, Two-Variable Statistics. In the dialogue box select studytime for the X list and grades for the Y List. [tab] to [OK] and press [enter].

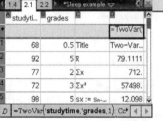

- Display the data in a scatterplot: Insert a Data & Statistics page. Press [tab] and Click to Add Variable on the horizontal axis will show the variables available. Select studytime for the horizontal axis. Press [tab] again and Click to Add Variable on the vertical axis will show the variables available. Select grades for the vertical axis.

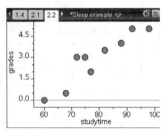

- Insert the least squares regression line: Press [menu], Analyze, Regression, Show Linear $(a + bx)$.

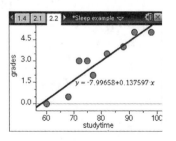

- Look at the residual plot to verify linearity of the model: Press menu, Analyze, Residuals, Show Residual Plot. The residual plot will appear below the scatterplot in a split window.

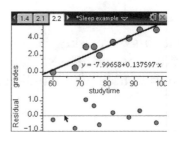

II. Sampling & Experimental Design

Selecting a Random Sample OR Random Assignment

You need to select 5 participants for a survey. There are 15 people available:

Adison	Bentley	Carter	Davids	Edwards
Francis	Granger	Hathaway	Ivers	Johnson
Keller	Lohman	Morris	Nance	Owens

- If you are given a list of individuals from which a sample is to be taken, the Nspire can randomly sample from this list, with OR without replacement.

- Insert a Lists & Spreadsheet page, and enter the subjects in the list.

BIG IDEA 4 On the AP Exam, it is unlikely that you would be expected to use a calculator to select a random sample. However, if you were, you could save precious time by numbering each subject and populating the list with these numbers.

1 – Adison	2 – Bentley	3 –Carter	4 – Davids	5 – Edwards
6 – Francis	7 – Granger	8 – Hathaway	9 – Ivers	10 – Johnson
11 – Keller	12 – Lohman	13 – Morris	14 – Nance	15 – Owens

- In a Lists & Spreadsheet page, name an empty column: subjects. Press enter twice, and in the formula bar type $\text{seq}(x,x,1,15)$. Then press enter again and the fifteen numbers should now be in the list.

In the next column, enter the name: sample. Press ⏎enter twice and in the formula bar type randsamp(subjects, 5, 1). Then press ⏎enter again and five numbers are chosen without replacement from subjects.

According to the random sample selection in the screen shot the following subjects were chosen for the sample: Granger, Carter, Hathaway, Johnson, and Morris.

III. Probability

A. Simulation

Some problems in statistics can be analyzed using simulation of a variable. We will look here at three of the Nspire's random number generators, each based on a specific distribution.

- To access the random number generators, go to the calculator scratchpad by pressing ⌨ or insert a Calculator page.

- Press menu, Probability, Random. A synopsis of the functions is listed below.

  → RandInt – this functions generates integers over a defined range.

  Command: randInt(lower bound, upper bound [, # of integers])

  Example: randInt(1, 28, 10) will produce 10 randomly selected integers between 1 and
      28, inclusive.

  → RandBin – this function generates values from a binomial distribution.

  Command: randBin(n, p, [# of values])
      n = number of trials
      p = probability of success on each trial

  Example: randBin(20, 0.2, 5) will produce 5 integers from a binomial distribution with 20 trials and a probability of success on each trial of 0.2.

  → RandNorm – this function generates values from a normal distribution.

  Command: randNorm(mean, standard deviation, [# of values])

  Example: randNorm(5, 2.1) will produce one value from a normal distribution with a mean of 5 and a standard deviation of 2.1.

In the last example, notice there is not a third value given in the command. If no value is given, the Nspire will assign the value 1 by default.

B. Distributions

- To calculate probabilities from given distributions, go to the calculator scratchpad by pressing ▭ or insert a Calculator page.

- Press menu, Statistics, Distributions. A synopsis of the functions is listed below with the dialogue box.

→ normCdf(lowBound, upBound, μ, σ) – calculates the probability of a normally distributed random variable with the mean and standard deviation specified lying between the lower and upper bounds entered.

→ invNorm(Area, μ, σ) – gives the particular value of a normally distributed random variable for a given area.

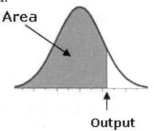

→ tCdf(lowBound,upBound,df) – calculates the probability of a t statistic lying in the given range for a t distribution with the number of degrees of freedom entered.

→ invt(Area, df) – gives the t statistic for a given probability for the number of degrees of freedom entered.

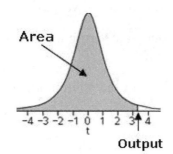

→ χ^2 Cdf(lowBound,upBound,df) – calculates the probability that a χ^2 statistic lies between the bounds entered, for the number of degrees of freedom specified.

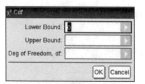

→ binomPdf(n, p, XVal) – calculates the probability that a particular number of successes, X, will occur, when there are n trials and the probability of success on each trial is p.

→ binomCdf(n, p, lowBound, upBound) – calculates the probability that the number of successes, X, will lie between lowbound and upbound (inclusive), when there are n trials and the probability of success on each trial is p.

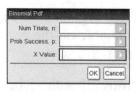

→ geomPdf(p, XVal) – calculates the probability that it takes X tries until a success for the entered probability of success, p.

→ geomCdf(p, lowBound, upBound) – calculates the probability that the number of trials to achieve a success, X, lies between lowBound and upBound (inclusive).

IV. Inference

A. Confidence Intervals

Press [menu], *Statistics*, *Confidence Intervals*

Each type of confidence interval calculation available on the Nspire is listed in the screen shot to the right.

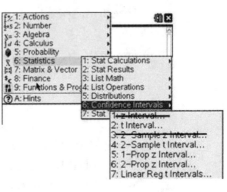

Notice that the *z* Interval and 2-Sample *z* Interval are crossed off. These calculations are unlikely to be necessary on the AP exam.

B. Hypothesis Tests

Press [menu], *Statistics*, *Stat Tests*.

Each type of hypothesis test that you have learned in AP Statistics is available on the Nspire and is listed in the screen shot to the right.

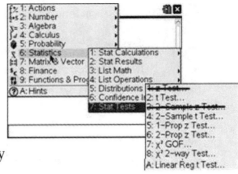

Notice that the *z* Test and 2-Sample *z* Test are crossed off. These tests are unlikely to be necessary on the AP exam since knowing the population standard deviation, σ, when the population mean is unknown, is unrealistic.

All of the inference procedures shown in the screenshots above are outlined on the formula sheet that is provided with the exam. In the next section, the formula sheet has been annotated with the appropriate commands for the Nspire. Further reminders and suggestions have also been included.

THE AP STATISTICS FORMULA SHEET AND ASSOCIATED TI-NSPIRE FUNCTIONALITY

To access the Stats menu: Press [menu] → Statistics

Below are the formulas that are provided with the AP exam. Additionally, descriptions are given as to how to access the associated functions on the Nspire.

I. Descriptive Statistics

One-variable

$$\bar{x} = \frac{\sum x_i}{n}$$
Mean of a data set

$$s_x = \sqrt{\frac{1}{n-1}\sum(x_i - \bar{x})^2}$$
Standard deviation of a data set

$$s_p = \sqrt{\frac{(n_1 - 1)\,s_1^2 + (n_2 - 1)\,s_2^2}{(n_1 - 1) + (n_2 - 1)}}$$
Pooled standard deviation for two samples (rarely required on the AP exam)

One-variable statistics:

Mean, standard deviation, five-number summary…

These numerical summaries are easiest to calculate in the *Lists & Spreadsheet* application.

Press [menu], *Statistics, Stat Calculations, One-Variable Statistics*.

Results

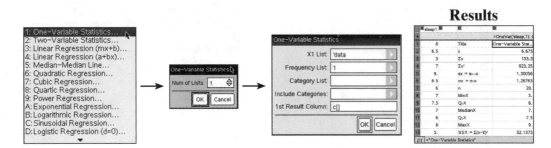

Two-variable

$\hat{y} = b_0 + b_1 x$ Equation of the least squares regression line

$b_1 = \dfrac{\sum (x_i - \bar{x})(y_i - \bar{y})}{\sum (x_i - \bar{x})^2}$ Slope of the LSRL

$b_0 = \bar{y} - b_1 \bar{x}$ y-intercept of the LSRL

$r = \dfrac{1}{n-1} \sum \left(\dfrac{x_i - \bar{x}}{s_x} \right) \left(\dfrac{y_i - \bar{y}}{s_y} \right)$ Correlation

$b_1 = r \dfrac{s_y}{s_x}$ Finding slope using correlation

$s_{b_1} = \dfrac{\sqrt{\dfrac{\sum (y_i - \hat{y}_i)^2}{n-2}}}{\sqrt{\sum (x_i - \bar{x})^2}}$ Standard error of the slope estimate

Two-Variable Statistics, Linear Regression; $\bar{x}, \bar{y}, r, \hat{y} \ldots$

The numerical summaries and linear regression equation for bivariate data are best calculated in the *Lists & Spreadsheet* application.

Press menu , *Statistics, Stat Calculations, Two-Variable Statistics* or *Linear Regression* $(a + bx)$.

Two Variable Statistics

Two-Variable Statistics	
X List:	'studytime
Y List:	'grades
Frequency List:	1
Category List:	
Include Categories:	
1st Result Column:	d[]

OK Cancel

	A studytime	B grades	C	D
				=TwoVar('studytime
1	0.5	68	Title	Two-Variable Sta...
2	5	92	x̄	2.88889
3	2	77	Σx	26.
4	3	72	Σx²	100.5
5	5	98	sx := sn-...	1.78146
6	0	60	σx := σnx...	1.67958
7	3	75	n	9.
8	3.5	82	ȳ	79.1111
9	4	88	Σy	712.
10			Σy²	57498.
11			sy := sn-...	12.098
12			σy := σny...	11.4061
13			Σxy	2218.
14			r	0.934428

D1 ="Two-Variable Statistics"

Linear Regression

Linear Regression (a+bx)	
X List:	'studytime
Y List:	'grades
Save RegEqn to:	f1
Frequency List:	1
Category List:	
Include Categories:	

OK Cancel

	A studytime	B grades	C	D	E	F
				=LinRegBx('s		
1	0.5	68	Title	Linear Regr...		
2	5	92	RegEqn...	a+b*x		
3	2	77	a	60.779		
4	3	72	b	6.34573		
5	5	98	r²	0.873156		
6	0	60	r	0.934428		
7	3	75	Resid	{4.0481400...		
8	3.5	82				
9	4	88				

D1 ="Linear Regression (a+bx)"

II. Probability

$$P(A \cup B) = P(A) + P(B) - P(A \cap B)$$
Probability that at least one of the events A, B occurs

$$P(A|B) = \frac{P(A \cap B)}{P(B)}$$
Probability that event A occurs given that B occurs

$$E(X) = \mu_x = \sum x_i p_i$$
Expected value of random variable X

$$\text{Var}(x) = \sigma_x^2 = \sum (x_i - \mu_x)^2 p_i$$
Variance of random variable X

REMEMBER: The expected value of the sum of any two random variables is the sum of the expected values of the two random variables, and the expected value of the difference of two random variables is the difference of their expected values. However, if two independent random variables are added or subtracted, their <u>variances</u> always ADD.
Example: $E(3X - 2Y) = 3E(X) - 2E(Y)$
$$\text{Var}(3X - 2Y) = 3^2 \text{Var}(X) + 2^2 \text{Var}(Y)$$

If X has a binomial distribution with parameters n and p, then:

$$P(X = k) = \binom{n}{k} p^k (1-p)^{n-k}$$

$$\mu_x = np$$

$$\sigma_x = \sqrt{np(1-p)}$$

$$\mu_{\hat{p}} = p$$

$$\sigma_{\hat{p}} = \sqrt{\frac{p(1-p)}{n}}$$

If $\overline{x}$ is the mean of a random sample of size n from an infinite population with mean μ and standard deviation σ, then:

$$\mu_{\overline{x}} = \mu$$

$$\sigma_{\overline{x}} = \frac{\sigma}{\sqrt{n}}$$

Binomial Probabilities:

WORDING CLUES: "What is the probability/chance that exactly # out of #..." OR "What is the probability that more than/at least/at most # out of #...?"

NOTE: On a free response question about the binomial distribution, it is fine to use binompdf or binomcdf. However, you should be sure to state the distribution and the parameters, and provide a calculation. For example, you could use binompdf(10,0.7,6) and write: "The distribution of the number of baskets scored is binomial, with $n = 10$ and $p = 0.7$. So the probability that the player makes a score of 6, using a calculator, is 0.200."

PROBABILITY CALCULATIONS:

Press menu, Probability, Distributions. The most frequently used distributions are binomial, normal, t, and χ^2.

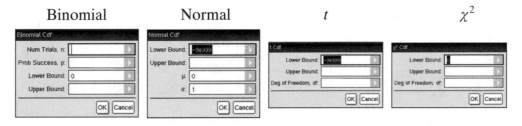

III. Inferential Statistics

Confidence interval:

Statistic ± (critical value) · (standard deviation of statistic)

Press $\boxed{\text{menu}}$, *Statistics, Confidence Intervals*

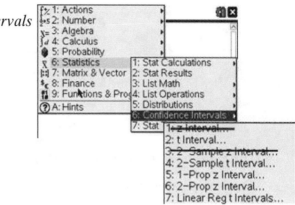

Calculator screens for confidence interval calculations

Proportions   Means

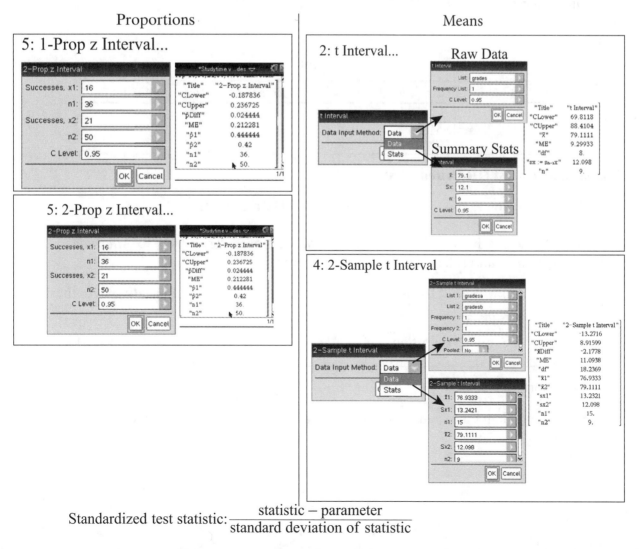

Standardized test statistic: $\dfrac{\text{statistic} - \text{parameter}}{\text{standard deviation of statistic}}$

Press menu , *Statistics, Stat Tests.*

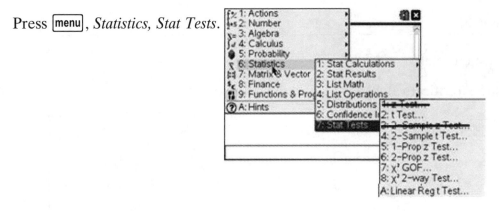

THESE FORMULAS ARE NOT ON THE FORMULA SHEET:

One-proportion z-test: $z = \dfrac{\hat{p} - p}{\sqrt{\dfrac{p(1-p)}{n}}}$

One-sample t-test: $t = \dfrac{\overline{x} - \mu}{\dfrac{s}{\sqrt{n}}}$

Single-Sample

Statistic	Standard Deviation of Statistic
Sample Mean	$\dfrac{\sigma}{\sqrt{n}}$

One-sample t-test OR Paired t-test

→ In the dialogue box, you will choose either **Data** or **Stats**

→ **Data**: Select the list where your *raw data* are stored. Then tab to *Alternate Hypothesis* and select the appropriate option.

→ **Stats**: You will need to enter $\overline{x}$, S_x, n, and the appropriate alternative hypothesis.

Sample Proportion	$\sqrt{\dfrac{p(1-p)}{n}}$

One-proportion z-test

→ In the dialogue box, enter *Successes, n,* and appropriate alternative hypothesis.

Two-Sample

Statistic	Standard Deviation of Statistic
Difference of Sample Means	$$\sqrt{\dfrac{\sigma_1^2}{n_1}+\dfrac{\sigma_2^2}{n_2}}$$ special case when $\sigma_1 = \sigma_2$ $$\sigma\sqrt{\dfrac{1}{n_1}+\dfrac{1}{n_2}}$$
Difference of Sample Proportions	$$\sqrt{\dfrac{p_1\,(1-p_1)}{n_1}+\dfrac{p_2\,(1-p_2)}{n_2}}$$ special case when $p_1 = p_2$ $$\sqrt{p\,(1-p)}\,\sqrt{\dfrac{1}{n_1}+\dfrac{1}{n_2}}$$

Two-sample t-test

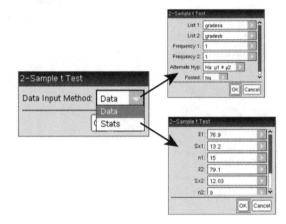

Two-proportion z-test

→ In the dialogue box, enter *Successes* and *n* for each proportion.

→ Select the appropriate alternative hypothesis.

χ^2-tests

Goodness of Fit:

- Enter your OBSERVED data into a column on a *Lists & Spreadsheet* page. (Be sure to name it.)

- Calculate the EXPECTED values and enter these into the next column. (Also name this one.)

- Press [menu], *Statistics, Stat Tests, χ^2 GOF*.

- Select your observed list by pressing [var] and arrowing up or down to the list name.

- Repeat the above step for the expected list.

- [tab] to OK and press [enter].

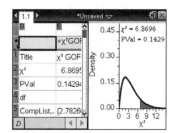

Two-Way Tables:

- On a *Calculator* page, define the OBSERVED matrix:

  o Enter a name, such as: **obs** [:=] (this symbol is obtained by pressing [ctrl] [⊟{⊟}]).

  o To enter the data into a matrix, press [⊟{⊟}]. In the dialogue box that appears, enter the number of rows and columns. [tab] to OK and press [enter]. A blank matrix should appear on the calculator page.

o Enter the data corresponding the rows and columns in the data table. When you are done, press ⌨enter.

$$genderparty = \begin{bmatrix} 94 & 78 & 18 \\ 88 & 86 & 36 \end{bmatrix}$$

- Press ⌨menu, *Statistics, Stat Tests*, χ^2 *2-way Test*. A dialogue box will appear asking for the *Observed Matrix*. Press ⌨var and select your observed matrix. ⌨tab to OK and press ⌨enter.

χ² 2-way Test

Observed Matrix: genderparty

OK Cancel

The results of your inference procedure will now be displayed. To view the *Expected Matrix*, press ⌨var and select **stat.expmatrix**.

χ²2way *genderparty*. *stat.results*

"Title"	"χ² 2-way Test"
"χ²"	5.60205
"PVal"	0.060748
"df"	2.
"ExpMatrix"	"[...]"
"CompMatrix"	"[...]"

Confidence Interval for the Slope of the Population Regression Line

- Enter the data into two lists on a *Lists & Spreadsheet* page.

- Insert a *Calculator* page.

- Press ⌨menu, *Statistics, Confidence Intervals, LinReg t Interval*.

o In the first dialogue box, select *slope*. ⌨tab to OK and press ⌨enter.

Linear Reg t Intervals

Interval: Slope

OK Cancel

o In the second dialogue box, select your *X* List and *Y* List. [tab] to [OK] and press [enter].

Linear Reg t Intervals	
X List:	xdata
Y List:	ydata
Save RegEqn to:	f1
Frequency List:	1
C Level:	0.95
	OK Cancel

o The results should now be displayed on the *Calculator* page.

"Title"	"Linear Reg t Test"
"Alternate Hyp"	"β & ρ ≠ 0"
"RegEqn"	"a+b*x"
"t"	6.94159
"PVal"	0.000223
"df"	7.
"a"	60.779
"b"	6.34573
"s"	4.60622
"SESlope"	0.914161
"r²"	0.873156
"r"	0.934428
"Resid"	"{...}"

Hypothesis Test for the Slope of the Population Regression Line

- Insert a *Calculator* page.

- Press [menu], *Statistics, Stat Tests, LinReg t Test.*

  o As with the confidence interval, select your *X List* variable, and your *Y List* variable in the dialogue box.

  o Select your alternative hypothesis, [tab] to [OK], and press [enter]. The results of the test will be displayed.

LinRegtTest *studytime,grades*,1,0: CopyVar

"Title"	"Linear Reg t Test"
"Alternate Hyp"	"β & ρ ≠ 0"
"RegEqn"	"a+b*x"
"t"	6.94159
"PVal"	0.000223
"df"	7.
"a"	60.779
"b"	6.34573
"s"	4.60622
"SESlope"	0.914161
"r²"	0.873156
"r"	0.934428
"Resid"	"{...}"

CALCULATOR-BASED SAMPLE QUESTIONS
AND THEIR SOLUTIONS

The following questions are examples of multiple choice problems such as those you might see on the AP exam that either require the use of a calculator or where the calculator helps you to answer the question quickly.

1. A certain company that sells high definition TVs is considering offering a 5-year guarantee for their current model. The probability distribution for the number of complete years a TV of this type will last is shown below.

Number of Complete Years	0	1	2	3	4	5	6	7	8	9
Probability	0.10	0.12	0.03	0.14	0.32	0.12	0.08	0.05	0.03	0.01

What is the expected number of complete years that a TV of this type will last?

(A) 0.60
(B) 1.10
(C) 2.5
(D) 3.64
(E) 4

2. In a random sample of 400 adults, each person stated his or her political preference. The gender (male/female) of each respondent was also noted. The results are shown in the table below:

	Democrat	Republican	Others
Male	94	78	18
Female	88	86	36

If a chi-square test for independence is performed, what would be the contribution to the statistic from the Female Democrats?

(A) 0.0001
(B) 0.5966
(C) 0.6594
(D) 2.0643
(E) 2.2816

3. A popular brand of cereal is including 3 different types of prizes. Each box contains one prize and the manufacturer has stated that, in any given box, the three prizes are equally likely. Claire wants one of the prizes and is surprised when she has to buy 5 boxes of cereal to get it. Assuming that the boxes are independent of each other in terms of the prizes they contain, what is the probability, when a person is waiting for a particular prize, that it takes at least 5 boxes for the prize to appear?

(A) 0.1975
(B) 0.3008
(C) 0.4489
(D) 0.6992
(E) 0.7985

4. The heights of the women in a particular community are normally distributed with a mean of 64.5 inches and a standard deviation of 2.5 inches. Thirty percent of women are taller than what height?

(A) 63.2 inches
(B) 65.0 inches
(C) 65.8 inches
(D) 67.0 inches
(E) 68.0 inches

5. A local appliance rental store offers only short-term rentals and "rent-to-own" rentals. For a number of years, roughly one half of the rentals have been short-term rentals. After a change in marketing strategy, the manager of the store examines the first 50 rentals and finds that 32 of them are short-term rentals. Treating these 50 rentals as a random sample of all rentals after the change in marketing strategy, the manager performs a hypothesis test to determine whether this result provides sufficient evidence that the proportion of all rentals that are short-term is now different from a half. Which of the following is closest to the p-value for this test?

(A) 0.005
(B) 0.048
(C) 0.096
(D) 0.230
(E) 0.396

Solutions

1. **(D) 3.64**

   This question requires you to calculate the mean of a random variable. This can be done using the *Lists & Spreadsheet* application of the TI-Nspire.

   - In a *Lists & Spreadsheet*, name column A: **year** and column B: **prob**.

   - Enter the data from the table in the appropriate columns.

   - Press menu, *Statistics, Stat Calculations, One-Variable Statistics*.

One-Variable Statistics	
X1 List:	year
Frequency List:	prob
Category List:	
Include Categories:	
1st Result Column:	d[]
	OK Cancel

   - Select **year** for the *X List* and **prob** for the *Frequency List*. Put the results in column d.

   - tab to OK and press enter. In the resulting display, your answer will be what is listed for $\bar{x}$.

1.1			*Unsaved ▽	
prob	C	D	E	
			=OneVar("	
1	0.1	Title	One-Var..	
2	0.12	x̄	3.64	
3	0.03	Σx	3.64	
4	0.14	Σx²	17.68	
5	0.32	sx := Sn-...	#UNDEF...	
E1	="One-Variable Statistics"		◀ ▶	

2. **(B) 0.5966**

   The Nspire will calculate a matrix with the contributions to the chi-square statistic.

   - On a *Calculator* page, define a matrix:

     - Type **genderparty**, and press ctrl := and then press ⊞.

       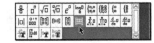

- Select 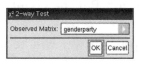 and enter 2 rows and 3 columns.

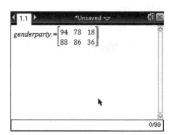

- Enter the data from the table in the matrix and press enter .

$$genderparty. = \begin{bmatrix} 94 & 78 & 18 \\ 88 & 86 & 36 \end{bmatrix}$$

- Press menu , *Statistics, Stat Tests, χ^2 2-way Test*.

  - In the dialogue box, select **genderparty** for the *Observed Matrix*.

  χ² 2-way Test
  Observed Matrix: genderparty
  OK Cancel

  - tab to OK and press enter .

  - The results of the test will be displayed.

  χ² 2way *genderparty. stat.results*

"Title"	"χ² 2-way Test"
"χ²"	5.60205
"PVal"	0.060748
"df"	2.
"ExpMatrix"	"[...]"
"CompMatrix"	"[...]"

  - To view the contributions (or component) matrix, press var and select **stat.compmatrix**.

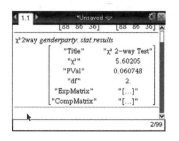

The contribution for female democrats

Note: If you have already performed stat functions, select the most recent **stat** variables.

3. **(A) 0.1975**

This question uses the geometric distribution, with $P(X \geq 5)$.

- On a calculator page, press menu, *Probability, Distributions, Geometric Cdf.*

- In the dialogue window that appears, type in the *Prob success p*: 1/3, *Lower Bound* 5, *Upper Bound* 10000 (a very large number).

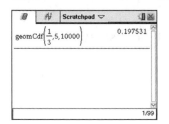

- tab to OK and press enter. The answer will be displayed.

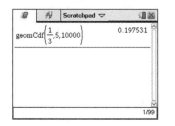

4. **(C) 65.8 inches**

Use of the Inverse Normal command will quickly determine the answer to this question. Note that the proportion of heights that are *less* than the required height is $1 - 0.30 = 0.70$.

- On a *Calculator* page, press menu, *Statistics, Distributions, Inverse Normal.*

- In the dialogue box, enter 0.7 for *Area*, 64.5 for μ, and 2.5 for σ. tab to OK and press enter.

- The answer will be displayed.

5. **(B) 0.048**

This question requires use of a 1-*proportion z-test*, with null hypothesis that the proportion of rentals that are short-term, p, is 0.5, and the alternative hypothesis that $p \neq 0.5$.

- On a *Calculator* page, press [menu], *Statistics, Stat Tests*, 1 *Prop Z Test*.

- In the dialogue box, type 0.5 for p_0, 32 for successes, x, 50 for n, and *prop $\neq$ p_0* for the alternate hypothesis.

```
1-Prop z Test
              P0:  0.5
    Successes, x:  32
              n:  50
   Alternate Hyp:  Ha: prop ≠ p0
                              OK  Cancel
```

- [tab] to OK and press [enter]. The results of the test will be displayed. The *p*-value is displayed beside "*PVal*".

```
1.1  1.2          *Unsaved ▽
zTest_1Prop 0.5,32,50,0: stat.results
          "Title"      "1-Prop z Test"
     "Alternate Hyp"    "prop ≠ p0"
            "z"            1.9799
           "PVal"         0.047715
            "p̂"           0.64
            "n"           50.

                              1/99
```

REVIEW EXERCISES

The exercises that follow cover the entire AP Statistics syllabus, and the questions include virtually all of the facts, knowledge, and skills that are required on the exam. It's a good idea initially to try to do the problems without using your class notes or a textbook, and then to use those resources to help you complete your work or to check your answers. Be sure, also, to refer to the Top Tips for the topic area you're working on. (The Top Tips start on page 1.)

Solutions to these review exercises are provided in the Student's Solutions Manual.

By working through these exercises, and by checking your answers in the Student's Solutions Manual, you'll greatly increase your knowledge and ability in AP Statistics. This could significantly improve your performance on the exam!

1. UNIVARIATE AND CATEGORICAL DATA

1.1

The stemplot below shows the number of counties for the fifty US states. (Key: 5|3 is a state with 53 counties.)

```
 0 | 3558
 1 | 044566
 2 | 1339
 3 | 0369
 4 | 46
 5 | 3568
 6 | 2446777
 7 | 257
 8 | 2378
 9 | 23559
10 | 025
11 | 4
12 | 0
13 |
14 |
15 | 9
16 |
17 |
18 |
19 |
20 |
21 |
22 |
23 |
24 |
25 | 4
```

(a) The state with the smallest number of counties is Delaware, which has 3 counties. The state with the largest number of counties is Texas. How many counties does Texas have?

(b) The mean and the standard deviation of the number of counties per state are 62.02 and 45.55, respectively. Explain how the value 45.55 summarizes the variability of the number of counties data.

(c) Without using a calculator, find the median, the lower and upper (first and third) quartiles, the interquartile range, and the range of this data set.

(d) Briefly describe the shape of the distribution.

(e) Are there any outliers in this data set? If so, which values are outliers? Show the calculations that lead to your answer.

(f) For describing the center and the spread of the data set, would you recommend using the mean and the standard deviation or the median and the interquartile range? Give a reason for your answer.

(g) Make a boxplot (showing outliers, if any) of the given data set.

(h) Suppose that Texas reduced its number of counties to 200. What effect will this change have on each of the following? (Circle your chosen answers.)

   i. The median will: increase / decrease / stay the same.

   ii. The upper quartile will: increase / decrease / stay the same.

   iii. The interquartile range will: increase / decrease / stay the same.

   iv. The range will: increase / decrease / stay the same.

   v. The mean will: increase / decrease / stay the same.

   vi. The standard deviation will: increase / decrease / stay the same.

(i) Suppose that plans are being made for a national conference. Each state will send a delegate from each county, along with three additional delegates. So, for example, states with 5, 8, and 10 counties will send 8, 11, and 13 delegates, respectively. For the new data set consisting of the numbers of delegates sent to the conference, what will be the mean, standard deviation, median, lower quartile, upper quartile, interquartile range, and range? Do not use a calculator. (Assume from this point on that the number of counties for Texas is as given in the original data set.)

(j) Suppose, instead, that every state will send two delegates for each county and no further delegates. For the new data set consisting of the number of delegates for each state, find the mean, standard deviation, median, lower quartile, upper quartile, interquartile range, and range. (If you use a calculator, use only the +, −, ×, or ÷ keys.)

1.2

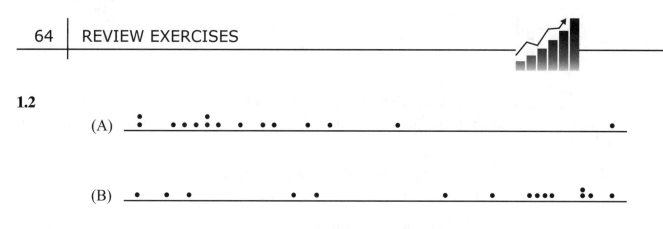

(A)

(B)

(a) Which of the dotplots above shows a distribution that is positively skewed?

(b) For the dotplot you chose, which will be greater, the mean or the median? Justify your answer.

1.3

In 2009, 53.7% of births in the U.S. were to Caucasian mothers, 14.8% were to African American mothers, 24.3% were to Hispanic mothers, and the remaining 7.2% of births were to mothers of other racial origins. Which one or more of the following could be used to display the distribution of birth mothers' racial origins?

(A) Bar graph

(B) Histogram

(C) Stemplot

(D) Boxplot

(E) Scatterplot

1.4

A study conducted on 500 men investigated the connection between left/right handedness and the age of the person's mother when he was born. The results are shown below.

	Mother's Age		
	Younger	Medium	Older
Left Handed	10	17	28
Right Handed	162	125	158
Total	172	142	186

(a) Copy and complete the table below.

	Mother's Age		
	Younger	Medium	Older
Percent Left Handed	6		
Percent Right Handed	94		

(b) Construct a graph that displays the relationship between age of mother and left/right handedness.

(c) What do parts (a) and/or (b) reveal about the relationship between mother's age at the person's birth and left/right handedness for the men in this sample?

1.5

Toby plans to buy a hybrid car. He found the fuel efficiencies (in miles per gallon) and the manufacturer's suggested retail price for seven cars on the Internet. These values, with the corresponding z-scores, are shown in the table below.

Model	Fuel Efficiency	Price	z-score for Fuel Efficiency	z-score for Price
A	30	34800	0.72	−0.49
B	25	22600	−0.01	
C	29	29600	0.57	−0.76
D	22	71400	−0.46	1.43
E	20	67500	−0.75	1.23
F	15	49400	−1.49	0.28
G	35	33600	1.46	−0.55
Mean	25.1	44100		
Standard Deviation	6.8	19100		

(a) Calculate the z-score for the price of Model B.

(b) Explain the meaning of the value you calculated in part (a).

(c) Toby is choosing between Models C and G. Based on the z-scores for the prices and fuel efficiencies of these two models, which of the two should he choose? (Assume that high fuel efficiencies and low prices are preferable.)

1.6

The cumulative relative frequency graph shown below displays the ages of the residents of a country.

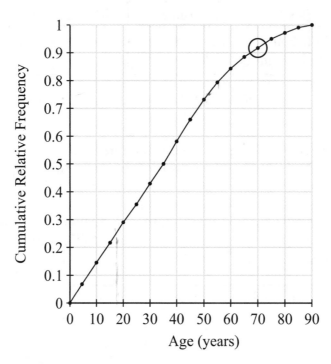

(a) What information is conveyed by the circled point?

(b) What is the median age for residents of this country?

(c) What is the interquartile range of the ages of this country's residents?

(d) The oldest 20% of residents will qualify for senior discounts. What is the minimum age required for senior discounts?

1.7

High density lipoprotein (HDL) cholesterol is often referred to as "good cholesterol" because high levels of HDL are thought to reduce the risk of a heart attack. The HDL levels (in milligrams per deciliter of blood) were measured for 52 people who exercise regularly and for 60 people who do not exercise regularly. The results are displayed in the histograms below.

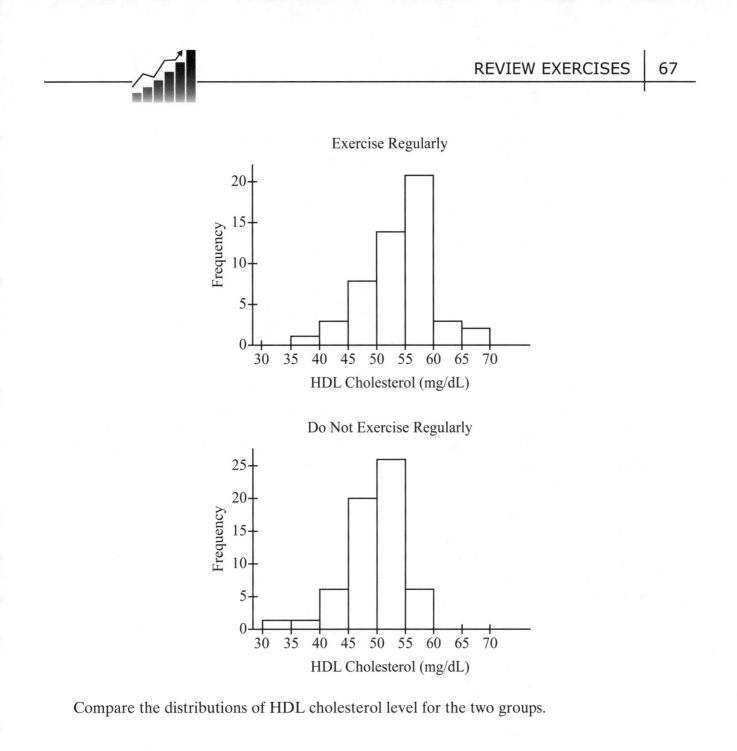

Compare the distributions of HDL cholesterol level for the two groups.

2. CORRELATION AND LINEAR REGRESSION

2.1

A league of college baseball teams calculates the park factors "Runs" and "Doubles" used in Major League Baseball. The scatterplot below shows the relationship between these two factors last season. Describe the association between these two variables.

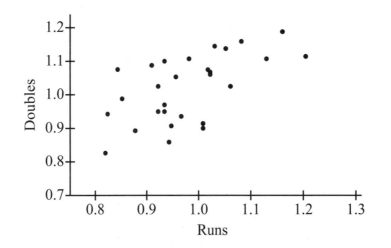

(Here's an explanation of what the "Runs" and "Doubles" variables mean: Suppose that Team X has a "Runs" value of 1.2. This number is greater than 1, which tells you that Team X's park is an easier park for scoring runs. Specifically, it tells you that Team X and its opponents are typically scoring more runs when playing at Team X's park than when they meet at Team X's opponents' parks. The "Doubles" variable is the same calculation applied to scoring doubles.)

2.2

A student at a large high school conducts a study using a random sample of 20 male seniors. The student records the height (in inches) and the length of the right foot (in millimeters) of each student selected, and uses a computer to fit a least squares regression line to the data. Part of the computer output is shown below.

```
Dependent variable: Foot Length

Predictor    Coef      SE Coef     T         P
Constant     148.17    42.88       3.46      0.003
Height       1.8849    0.5964      3.16      0.005

S = 6.85709     R-sq = 35.7%    R-sq (adj) = 32.1%
```

(a) What is the value of the correlation coefficient for foot length and height?

(b) Interpret the value of the correlation coefficient that you calculated in part (a).

(c) What is the equation of the least squares regression line for predicting foot length from height?

(d) A scatterplot of the results is shown below. Draw the least squares regression line on the scatterplot.

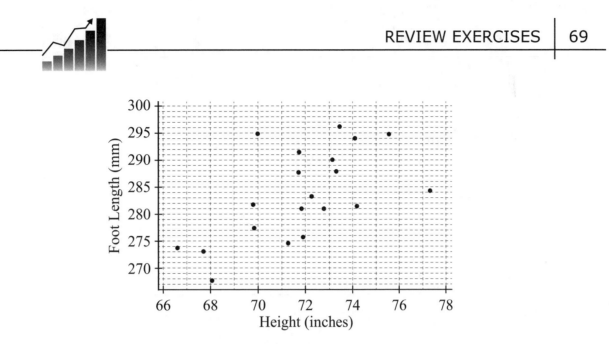

(e) Interpret the value of the slope of the least squares regression line in this context.

(f) Does the intercept of the least squares regression line have a meaningful interpretation in this context? If so, provide this interpretation. If not, explain why not.

(g) What does the least squares regression line predict for the foot length of a student whose height is 73 inches?

(h) Would it be appropriate to use the fitted regression equation to predict the foot length for a student whose height is 62 inches? Explain your answer.

(i) One of the students in the study had a height of 71.8 inches and a foot length of 291.5 millimeters. Calculate the residual for that student.

(j) Interpret the value of the residual you calculated in part (i).

(k) A residual plot for this data set is shown below.

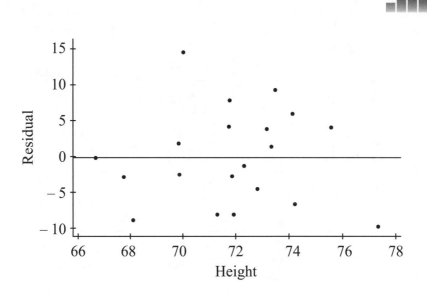

Is a line an appropriate model for the heights and foot lengths of these students? Explain how your reach your conclusion.

(l) State the value of r^2, and interpret this value in the context of this study.

(m) Note that $s = 6.85709$ in the computer output. Interpret this value in the context of this study.

(n) Identify and interpret the standard error of the slope.

(o) Suppose that a system of shoe sizes is formulated, where

$$\text{shoe size} = \frac{(\text{foot length}) - 285}{5}$$

If, using this formula, the foot length is replaced by the shoe size for each student (with no rounding), what would be the resulting value of the correlation coefficient for shoe size and height?

2.3

Suppose that the heights and foot lengths of 15 high school senior girls are measured. The heights are found to have mean 63.8 inches and standard deviation 4.2 inches and the foot lengths are found to have mean 223.3 millimeters and standard deviation 12.7 millimeters. Additionally, the correlation between height and foot length for these girls is found to be 0.548. Let x = height in inches and y = foot length in millimeters.

(a) Calculate the slope of the least squares regression line of y on x.

(b) Calculate the y-intercept of the least squares regression line of y on x.

2.4

(a) Consider the data set represented by the scatterplot shown below.

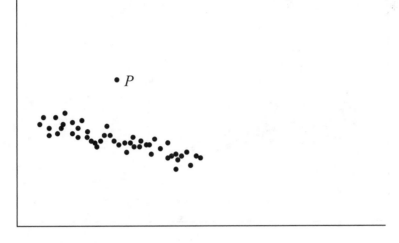

Would removal of the point *P* result in a large change in the least squares regression line? Explain your answer.

(b) Consider the data set represented by the scatterplot shown below.

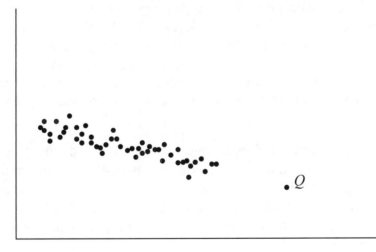

Would removal of the point *Q* result in a large change in the least squares regression line? Explain your answer.

(c) Consider the data set represented by the scatterplot shown below.

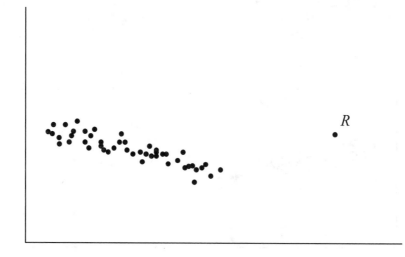

Would removal of the point R result in a large change in the least squares regression line? Explain your answer.

3. OBSERVATIONAL STUDIES AND EXPERIMENTS

3.1

(a) A study was conducted over a period of 16 years using a large number of adult males. The study concluded that men who often skipped breakfast were significantly more likely to suffer from heart disease later in life than those who regularly ate breakfast.
  i. Explain why this was an observational study, not an experiment.
  ii. Explain why you cannot conclude from the result of this study that, for men like these, skipping breakfast *causes* heart disease. Include a feasible confounding variable in your answer.

(b) Suppose that a study is conducted using mice. By random assignment, some of the mice receive a morning feed each day over an extended period; the remaining mice do not receive the morning feed. The mice that do not receive the morning feed are found to live significantly less long, on average, than the mice that do. Explain why you *can* conclude from this study that denying mice like these the morning feed causes them to die sooner.

3.2

A team of researchers is planning a study of the levels of experience among primary school teachers in a developing country. Each teacher selected to take part in the study will be interviewed and will fill out a detailed questionnaire. There are 3,054 primary school teachers in the country that is being studied.

(a) Explain why a census of teachers would not be practical.

(b) An easy way to conduct the study would be to include all of the large number of primary school teachers in the county's capital city. Why might this sampling method be biased in assessing the levels of experience of primary school teachers in the country?

(c) Suppose that the researchers have a computer list of all 3,054 primary school teachers. How might they use a computer to randomly select 200 of the teachers?

(d) One of the researchers suggests using a stratified random sample, stratifying by grade. In the country being studied, primary school consists of Grades 1 through 4.
   i. Provide an example of how the researchers might select a stratified random sample of 80 teachers, stratifying by grade.
   ii. What needs to be true about the teachers of the four grades so that it would be worthwhile to stratify by grade?
   iii. If your answer to part (ii) is true, why might this stratified random sampling process be preferable to selecting a simple random sample of 80 teachers?

(e) Another researcher suggests using cluster sampling, where the clusters are the country's 295 primary schools.
   i. Explain how a cluster sample of teachers from 10 schools could be selected.
   ii. What is the primary advantage of using this cluster sampling method over the simple random sampling described in part (b)?

3.3

A recent environmental demonstration in Washington, D.C. was covered on several national TV networks. In order to investigate people's reactions to the TV news coverage, a survey was made available to users of Internet news sites. The survey asked, "How do you feel about the negative images displayed in the TV coverage of the recent environmental demonstration?" On the basis of the results of the survey, "widespread displeasure" with the TV coverage was reported.

Describe three possible sources of bias in this survey. For each source of bias, explain how the bias might affect the estimate of the proportion of people who were unhappy with the TV coverage of the demonstration, and why the bias might have that effect.

3.4

An experiment is to be designed to compare two drugs, Drug A and Drug B, both designed to reduce blood pressure. (Drug A is a new formulation. Drug B is a formulation that has been used for some years.) You have been provided with 40 volunteers, all of whom suffer from high blood pressure. Twenty of the volunteers will receive Drug A, and the other 20 will receive Drug B. The reduction in blood pressure will be measured for each participant.

(a) Explain how the 40 volunteers might be randomly assigned to the two groups.

(b) Why would the volunteers be assigned *randomly* to the two groups, rather than, for example, allowing each volunteer (independently of the other volunteers) to choose which group he/she would be in?

(c) Suppose the blood pressures of the volunteers who are given Drug A are reduced significantly more, on average, than the blood pressures of the volunteers who are given Drug B. Explain why we have evidence that Drug A *causes* a greater reduction in blood pressure than Drug B does.

3.5

Suppose, now, that an experiment is designed to determine the effects of a particular drug <u>and</u> of exercising on people's blood pressures. Each participant will be given no drug at all, or 2mg per day of the drug, or 10 mg per day of the drug. Also, each participant will either exercise or not exercise. The reduction in blood pressure will be measured for each person who takes part in the experiment.

(a) What is/are the explanatory variable(s) in this experiment?

(b) What is/are the response variable(s) in this experiment?

(c) For each explanatory variable, how many levels are there?

(d) How many treatments are there?

(e) What/who are the experimental units in this context?

3.6

Consider an experiment to determine whether regular exercise, over an extended period, reduces blood pressure. A substantial number of volunteers who suffer from high blood pressure and who do not, as yet, exercise regularly will be used in the experiment.

(a) Suppose that all the participants in the experiment are given daily sessions of supervised exercise over a period of four months, and that their blood pressures are, on average, significantly reduced. Explain why this result does <u>not</u> give us evidence that regular exercise reduces blood pressure.

(b) Suppose now that the experiment is adapted so that the participants are randomly assigned to two groups. The participants in one of the groups are given the supervised daily exercise, while those in the other group (the control group) do not exercise. How does the inclusion of the control group solve the problem described in part (a)?

3.7

Consider an experiment in which a single drug, designed to reduce blood pressure, is being tested. The participants (all of whom suffer from high blood pressure) are randomly assigned to two groups: Group A and Group B. The participants in Group A will receive the drug.

(a) Suppose that the participants assigned to Group B are given no treatment at all, and that the participants in Group A undergo a significantly greater reduction in blood pressure than the participants in Group B. Explain why this does not give us evidence that the drug is effective.

(b) What, in the context of this experiment, is a placebo? Explain how use of a placebo for Group B overcomes the problem described in part (a) of this question.

3.8

An experiment is designed to compare three different fertilizers, Fertilizer A, Fertilizer B, and Fertilizer C, for the growth of potted plants of a particular species. A number of very similar young plants of this species are planted in soil in identical pots. Some of the pots are treated using Fertilizer A, some using Fertilizer B, and some using Fertilizer C. At the end of the experiment the grown plants are compared using a measure of quality that includes considerations such as the number of flowers, the number of leaves, and other aspects of the health of the plant.

(a) What is the explanatory variable in this experiment?

(b) What is the response variable?

(c) A lurking (extraneous) variable is a variable that is not the explanatory variable (or the response variable), but that nonetheless might have an effect on the response variable. List three possible lurking variables in the context of this experiment.

(d) Choose one of the lurking variables you provided in part (c), and explain what would need to be the case for this variable to be described as a *confounding* variable.

3.9

Return to the experiment described in Question 3.4, and assume that the 40 volunteers (who all suffered from high blood pressure) were randomly assigned to receive either Drug A or Drug B. Suppose that the blood pressures of the volunteers who were given Drug A were reduced significantly more, on average, than the blood pressures of those who were given Drug B. Can we conclude that Drug A would be more effective than Drug B for all patients who suffer from high blood pressure? Explain your answer.

3.10

(a) It has been suggested that the application of lemon juice or vinegar to a sliced avocado can prevent discoloration. Suppose that you have been provided with 30 half avocadoes, recently cut. Describe a completely randomized experiment to determine which, of lemon juice or vinegar, is more effective for reducing discoloration. (Do not include a control group.)

(a) How might the experiment described in part (a) be adapted in order to make use of a matched pairs design? (Be sure to explain how the treatments would be assigned.)

(b) Why is a matched pairs design preferable to the design in part (a)?

3.11

    (a) Return, again, to the experiment described in Question 3.4 where a new drug (Drug A) is compared to a current drug (Drug B), and where both drugs are designed to reduce blood pressure. A number of volunteers who suffer from high blood pressure will be randomly assigned to receive either Drug A or Drug B.

        i. What two criteria are required for the experiment to be described as "double blind"?
        ii. Explain why the two criteria you provided in part (a) are important in this experiment.
        iii. What would need to be the case for the experiment to be described as "single blind"?

    (b) Suppose an experiment were to be designed to determine the effect of regular exercise on people's blood pressure. Explain why a double blind design is not possible for this experiment.

3.12

A statistics teacher wants to compare three different teaching methods: Method A, Method B, and Method C. She decides to use her class of 18 students. Completely randomly, she will assign 6 students to Method A, 6 to Method B, and 6 to Method C. The students will be taught the same topic using these methods, and they will then all be given the same test. The three methods will be compared by comparing the average test results for the three groups.

What problem might arise as a result of using as few as 6 students in each treatment group? Explain why using a larger class of 42 students, for example (and therefore having 14 students in each treatment group), would be preferable.

(This question provides an example of the need for adequate *replication*.)

3.13

Return to the scenario described in the previous question, where the teacher wishes to compare the three teaching methods using her class of 18 students.

    (a) The teacher has a list of all the students' average scores in her course up to the time when she is going to start the experiment. Explain how she would conduct this experiment using blocking by average grade in the course. Use blocks of size three, and be sure to include a detailed explanation as to how the treatments would be assigned.

(b) Explain why the block design is preferable to the completely randomized design described in the previous question.

4. PROBABILITY

4.1

A music enthusiast has a collection of vintage recorded music consisting of 3390 albums. Each album has been classified as one of classical, jazz, or popular, and is on either CD, vinyl, or cassette.

(There is only one recording of each album in the collection.) The numbers of albums falling into these categories are given in the table below.

	CD	Vinyl	Cassette	Total
Classical	846	690	81	1617
Jazz	693	562	116	1371
Popular	158	95	149	402
Total	1697	1347	346	3390

(a) An album is chosen at random from this collection. Find the probability that it is
    i. jazz
    ii. jazz and on vinyl
    iii. jazz or on vinyl
    iv. jazz, given that it is on vinyl

When an album is chosen at random from the collection, let J be the event that it is jazz and let V be the event that it is on vinyl.

(b) Are J and V mutually exclusive events?

(c) Are J and V independent events?

4.2

In a particular community, 80% of the people wear deodorant, 40% exercise regularly, and 84% do at least one of these two things.

(a) If a person is chosen at random from this community, what is the probability that the person wears deodorant and exercises regularly?

(b) If a person is chosen at random from this community, what is the probability that the person neither wears deodorant nor exercises regularly?

(c) What is the probability that a person in this community wears deodorant given that he/she exercises regularly?

(d) If a person is known not to wear deodorant, what is the probability that the person exercises regularly?

(e) In this community, are the events "wears deodorant" and "exercises regularly" mutually exclusive? Explain.

(f) In this community, are the events "wears deodorant" and "exercises regularly" independent? Explain.

(g) In a random sample of 1000 people from this community, how many would you expect to wear deodorant? Would <u>exactly</u> this number of people in the sample wear deodorant?

4.3

A student is about to take APs in US History, English Language, and Statistics. She estimates that her probabilities of getting 5's in these subjects are 0.6, 0.7, and 0.8, respectively. She is also willing to assume that her results in the three subjects are independent. Assuming that the student's estimates are correct, find the probability that she gets

(a) 5's in all three subjects

(b) no 5's

(c) exactly one 5

(d) at least one 5

4.4

A student named Lenny rides a bicycle to school on 3/5 of days, and on the other days is driven to school by car. When he uses the bicycle he is able to avoid traffic, and is on time to school with probability 0.95. When he is driven to school he is on time with probability 0.75.

(a) Complete the tree diagram below by writing the specified probabilities in the boxes.
   i. The probability that, on a randomly chosen day, Lenny rides his bicycle to school
   ii. The probability that, on a randomly chosen day, Lenny is driven to school
   iii. The probability that Lenny is on time, given that he rides his bicycle to school
   iv. The probability that Lenny is late, given that he rides his bicycle to school
   v. The probability that Lenny is on time, given that he is driven to school
   vi. The probability that Lenny is late, given that he is driven to school

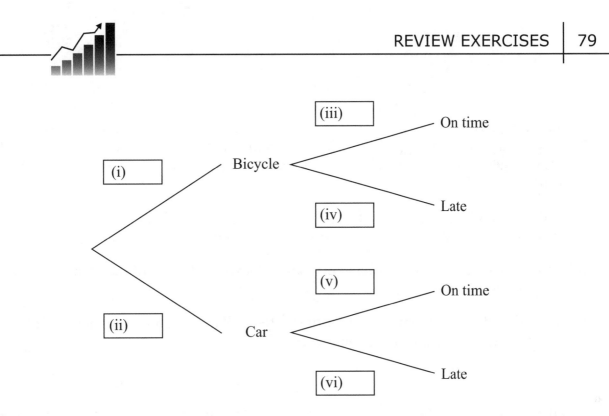

(b) If a day is chosen at random, what is the probability that, on that day, Lenny rides his bicycle to school and is on time?

(c) On what proportion of days is Lenny on time?

(d) If, on a particular day, Lenny is observed to be on time, what is the probability that Lenny rode his bicycle to school on that day?

4.5

A statistics teacher has 7 girls and 5 boys in her class. If the teacher chooses three students at random to record the results of a study, what is the probability that all three students are girls?

5. SIMULATION

5.1

(a) For a computer system that is being developed, a mathematician has estimated that the probability the system will crash when it is started is 48/913. Explain how you would use a table of random digits to simulate 20 starts of this computer system.

(b) There are 840 students in a high school. Explain how you would use a table of random digits to randomly select 20 students from the school.

5.2

A small company has 68 employees, of whom 40 are employed full time and the remaining 28 are part time. Fifteen employees will be selected at random to attend a convention. The director of the company is interested in the number of part time employees who will be selected.

(a) Explain how you would use a table of random digits to simulate the process of selecting a random sample of 15 employees and noting the number of part-time employees selected.

(b) How would you use simulation to estimate the expected value of the number of part-time employees selected?

(c) How would you use simulation to estimate the probability that more than half of the people selected are part-time employees?

5.3

Freddie has made a spinner. The spinner has a pointer, and when the pointer is spun, the possible outcomes are "red," "green," "yellow" and "blue". In order to test the spinner, Freddie spins the pointer 20 times, and notices that on 9 of these spins the outcome is "red". Freddie wants to know whether this result gives convincing evidence that the probability of "red" for his spinner is greater than 1/4.

Freddie asks his sister, Florence, who is taking AP Statistics. Florence designs a computer simulation of a theoretical spinner for which the probability of "red" is 1/4. Each run of the simulation consists of 20 spins of the theoretical spinner, and the computer records the number of reds for the 20 spins. Florence has the computer do 600 runs of the simulation, and the number of reds was greater than or equal to 9 in exactly 25 of these runs.

(a) Florence's simulation was for a theoretical spinner where the probability of "red" is 1/4. According to the results of her simulation, what is the approximate probability that 20 spins of this spinner will result in 9 or more reds?

(b) Does Freddie's result provide convincing evidence that the probability of "red" for his spinner is greater than 1/4? Use your answer to part (a), and explain your argument fully.

6. RANDOM VARIABLES

6.1

As part of its census, a country keeps record of the number of vehicles available to each household. Using this information, it is calculated that, when a household is chosen at random from the country, the probability distribution of the number of vehicles available is as shown below.

Number of Vehicles	0	1	2	3
Probability	0.32	0.42	0.17	0.09

(a) Calculate the mean number of vehicles per household in this country.

(b) Calculate the standard deviation of the number of vehicles available to households.

(c) The unit of currency for the country is the guilder. The government imposes a monthly tax of 320 guilders per household, plus 180 guilders for each vehicle available to the household. Using your answers to parts (a) and (b), calculate the mean and the standard deviation of the monthly tax amount (in guilders) for a randomly chosen household.

6.2

Jenna has started a business selling half-liter bottles of spring water. She sells the water using two methods. The first is through a small stall set up at a popular tourist location, where she sells individual bottles for cash. The second is through a web site, where customers can order cases of the bottles for local delivery. The number of bottles that she sells from the stall on a randomly selected day has mean 128 and standard deviation 16. The number of bottles she sells via the web site on a randomly selected day has mean 223 and standard deviation 35.

(a) Calculate the expected value of the total number of bottles sold on a randomly selected day.

(b) What assumption do you need to make in order to use the information given above to calculate the standard deviation of the total number of bottles sold on a randomly selected day? Do you consider this assumption to be reasonable? Explain.

In the questions that follow, assume that the assumption in part (b) holds.

(c) Calculate the standard deviation of the total number of bottles sold on a randomly selected day.

(d) Calculate the mean and the standard deviation of the amount by which, on a randomly selected day, the number of bottles sold through the web site exceeds the number of bottles sold from the stall.

(e) Jenna charges $1.25 per bottle at the stall and $0.57 per bottle on the web site. Calculate the mean and the standard deviation of the total amount of money she takes on a randomly selected day.

6.3

Nick plays basketball. When Nick takes a free throw, the probability that he is successful is 0.7. Today, Nick will take six free throws. Assuming that the outcomes of the throws are independent of each other, find the probability that he has

(a) exactly four successes

(b) at least four successes

6.4

Nick's younger brother, James, also plays basketball. For James, the probability of being successful on a free throw is 0.35. Suppose that James will take 10 free throws and that the outcomes of the throws are independent of each other.

(a) Find the probability that James has
  i. no successes
  ii. at least one success
  iii. at least three successes

(b) What are the mean and the standard deviation of the number of successes for James?

6.5

The basketball player in the previous question, James, decides to start taking free throws, and to continue until he gets his first success. Find the probability that the number of throws he takes up to and including his first success is

(a) three

(b) less than three

(c) more than three

6.6

In a particular population of polar bears, the adult males have masses that are normally distributed with mean 515 kilograms and standard deviation 88 kilograms.

(a) An adult male is chosen at random from this population. Calculate the probability that his mass is

i. between 480 and 580 kilograms

ii. less than 600 kilograms

iii. more than 450 kilograms

(b) What is the minimum mass required for a bear to be amongst the heaviest 20% of adult males in this population?

6.7

For a population of polar bears, 22% of the adult females have masses less than 240 kilograms. If the masses of adult females are known to be normally distributed with standard deviation 51 kilograms, what is the mean mass of adult females in this population?

6.8

For each of the following, say whether the distribution of the random variable X is most likely to be binomial, geometric, normal, or none of these. ("None of these" is allowed in only one answer.)

(a) You stand on a street in New York City and watch people using their cell phones. X is the number of phones out of the next ten that are smart phones.

(b) X is the number of flips of a coin until you get a head.

(c) X is the length of the next French fry that you eat.

(d) X is the number of journeys that you make to school up to the first viewing of a car with its trunk not fully closed.

(e) X is the score when a cube with faces numbered 1 through 6 is rolled.

(f) You know how many coins there are in your pocket. X is the number of heads that show when you drop all the coins on the floor.

7. SAMPLING DISTRIBUTIONS

7.1

A statistician needs to estimate the value of a parameter from a population. (For example, the parameter could be the population mean, the population third quartile, or the population interquartile range.) She has a choice of three different sample statistics to use, which we will call Statistic 1, Statistic 2, and Statistic 3. In order to compare the three statistics, the statistician constructs a computer model of the population, as she believes the population to be. She then uses the computer to randomly select many different samples of size 200 from the simulated population. For each sample the computer calculates the values of Statistic 1, Statistic 2, and Statistic 3. Parallel dotplots of the results are shown below. (Note that the three dotplots share a single scale, with the true location of the parameter as shown.)

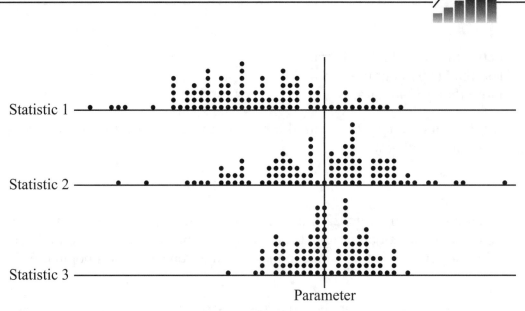

(a) Which of Statistic 1 and Statistic 2 is preferable? Explain your answer.

(b) Which of Statistic 2 and Statistic 3 is preferable? Explain your answer.

7.2

Helen is serving bowls of soup in a cafeteria. The amount of soup she serves per bowl has mean 12.0 ounces and standard deviation 1.1 ounces.

(a) Assuming that the amount of soup per bowl is normally distributed, calculate the probability that
   i. the mean amount of soup in 5 randomly selected bowls is between 11.5 and 12.5 ounces
   ii. the total amount of soup in 10 randomly selected bowls is greater than 128 ounces

(b) Suppose now that you cannot assume that the amount of soup per bowl is normally distributed.
   i. When will the mean amount of soup in a random sample of bowls nonetheless be approximately normally distributed? What is the name of the theorem that tells us this?
   ii. Calculate the probability that the mean amount of soup in 40 randomly selected bowls is less than 11.8 ounces.

7.3

A factory is manufacturing toy dogs. It is known that 5% of the completed dogs have defects.

(a) For a sufficiently large random sample of dogs we can assume that the sampling distribution of the sample proportion of defective dogs is approximately normal. How large does the random sample have to be in order for this assumption to be justified?

(b) A random sample of 300 dogs is selected. Calculate the approximate probability that less than 4% of the dogs in the sample are defective.

8. STATISTICAL INFERENCE

In questions 8.1–8.9, as a <u>first exercise</u> simply state the type of hypothesis test that is required. As a <u>second exercise</u>, perform all the tests.

8.1

A large pine forest is populated by three different types of pine tree: Sand Pine, Shortleaf Pine, and Loblolly Pine. It is known that 58% of the trees in the forest are Sand Pines, 22% are Shortleaf Pines, and 20% are Loblolly Pines. A random sample of 100 trees is selected from one region of the forest, and these 100 trees are categorized according to type, with the results as shown below.

Type of Pine	Sand	Shortleaf	Loblolly
Number of Trees	55	14	11

Does this sample provide convincing evidence that the proportions of the three types of pine are different in this region of the forest from the proportions in the forest as a whole?

8.2

The owners of a supermarket chain are interested in promoting fruit for its health-giving properties. As a pilot study, a random sample of 200 customers is selected, and each customer in the sample is asked whether he/she believes that eating oranges is good for your health. Of these 200 customers, 186 reply "Yes," with the remainder replying "No." Does this result provide convincing evidence that more than 90% of all customers would answer "Yes" to the question?

8.3

Ten years ago, a survey was conducted at a large college using a random sample of 140 students. Each student was asked "If you get a poor grade and have to tell a parent, do you tell him/her by email, by phone, or do you leave it until you next see him/her in person?" A similar survey was conducted at the same college five years ago using a random sample of 119 students, and again, this year, using a random sample of 132 students. The responses to the three surveys are summarized in the table below.

	10 Years Ago	5 Years Ago	This Year
Email	13	44	64
Phone	90	45	43
In Person	37	30	25

Do these results provide convincing evidence of any difference between the populations for the three different years in terms of the distribution of preferred mode of communication?

8.4

At a large high school for academically talented students, a random sample of 15 students was selected to take a mathematical problem-solving contest in two consecutive years. The scores for the 15 students are given below.

Student	1	2	3	4	5	6	7	8	9	10	11	12	13	14	15
Last Year	84	80	95	83	77	84	55	86	95	102	72	96	80	87	64
This Year	91	89	79	81	91	81	74	101	107	90	60	98	85	65	99

Do these results provide convincing evidence that, if all the students at the school had taken the contest on both occasions, this year's mean score would have been greater than last year's?

8.5

Do the results in the previous question provide convincing evidence of a useful linear relationship between last year's scores and this year's scores?

8.6

At a different school from the one described in Question 8.4, a random sample of 10 students was selected to take the math contest last year, and a different random sample of 10 students was selected to take the contest this year. The results are shown below.

Last Year	74	60	82	82	104	93	73	94	82	94
This Year	94	93	111	88	99	97	96	101	73	84

Do these results provide convincing evidence that, if all the students who were at the school last year had taken the contest and all the students who were at the school this year had taken the contest, this year's mean score would have been greater than last year's?

8.7

Refer to the information given in the previous question. Do last year's results provide convincing evidence that, if all the students at this school had taken the contest last year, the mean score would have been less than 90?

8.8

In a random sample of 165 men in long-term relationships, 32 said that they had bought valentines cards for their partners. In a random sample of 178 women in long-term relationships, 52 said that they had bought valentines cards for their partners. Do these results provide sufficient evidence to conclude that men and women in long-term relationships are different in terms of the proportions who would say that they bought valentines cards for their partners?

8.9

A large school district offers two buses on all its routes: an early bus and a late bus. On any given morning the students are free to decide which bus to take. Some take the early bus, as it covers the route more quickly and enables the student to take part in morning activities; others take the late bus as it gives them a small amount of extra sleep. On a particular day, a random sample of 350 high school students was selected. Each student was asked which bus he/she took, and the student's grade level was noted. The numbers of students falling into the various categories were as shown below.

	9	10	11	12
Early	56	48	38	83
Late	39	52	46	64

Do these results provide convincing evidence of an association between grade level and choice of bus for high school students in the district?

8.10

Explain, in the context of the question, the meaning of the *p*-value for the hypothesis test in

(a) Question 8.2

(b) Question 8.3

(c) Question 8.5

(d) Question 8.7

8.11

The *t*-test for a difference in population means and the *z*-test for a difference in population proportions can both be used to compare the results of independent random samples selected from two populations. What is the other scenario in which these two tests can be used? In what way(s) will your answer be different in this other scenario?

8.12

Refer to the information given in Question 8.2.

(a) Use the results of the study to construct a 95% confidence interval for the proportion of all customers who would answer "Yes" to the question.

(b) Explain the meaning of 95% confidence in this context.

8.13

Refer to the information given in Question 8.4. Use the results for the 15 students in the sample to construct a 90% confidence interval for the mean difference in score between the two years for all students at the school, if all students at the school had taken the contest on both occasions.

8.14

Refer once more to the information given in Question 8.4. Use the results for the 15 students in the sample to construct a 99% confidence interval for the slope of the regression line relating this year's score to last year's score for all students at the school, if all students at the school had taken the contest on both occasions. (You are given that the standard error of the slope, SE_b, or s_b, for this data set is 0.279.)

8.15

Refer to the information given in Question 8.6. Construct a 95% confidence interval for the difference in mean scores between the two years for all students at the school, if, on each occasion, all the students at the school at that time had taken the contest.

8.16

Refer again to the information given in Question 8.6. Construct a 99% confidence interval for the mean score last year for all students at the school, if all students at the school had taken the contest last year.

8.17

Refer to the information given in Question 8.8. Use the results given to construct a 90% confidence interval for the difference in the proportions of men and women in long-term relationships who would say that they bought valentines cards for their partners.

8.18

A researcher wishes to estimate the proportion of adults in a large city who have seen a particular commercial.

(a) How large a sample is required in order to estimate this proportion to within 0.02 with 99% confidence? Justify your answer.

(b) Suppose now that a pilot survey has estimated that 85% of adults in the city have seen the commercial. Using this estimate, how large a sample is required in order to estimate the actual proportion of adults in the city who have seen the commercial to within 0.02 with 99% confidence? Justify your answer.

8.19

A random sample of Brand A light bulbs and a random sample of Brand B light bulbs were selected. The lifetime (in hours) of each light bulb was determined, and the results were used to construct a 95% confidence interval for the mean lifetime of all Brand A light bulbs minus the mean lifetime of all Brand B light bulbs. The confidence interval was (−29.74, 56.85). Is there convincing evidence that the mean lifetimes of Brand A and Brand B light bulbs are different? Explain your answer.

8.20

A factory produces smoke alarms. For an extended period, faults have been found in only one in every thousand smoke alarms produced. However, the factory's machinery has recently been overhauled, and the management has decided to test the product. A random sample of smoke alarms will be selected and tested, and if there is convincing evidence that the proportion of alarms that are defective is greater than 0.001, the machinery will be inspected in order to find out what is causing the greater proportion of defective alarms.

Let p be the true proportion of defective alarms.

(a) Write the null and alternative hypotheses that will be used for the hypothesis test.

(b) Describe a Type I error in this context. What would be the consequences of a Type I error?

(c) Describe a Type II error in this context. What would be the consequences of a Type II error?

(d) A decision has to be made as to whether a 1% or 5% significance level will be used for the hypothesis test. Which of these significance levels will produce the smaller probability of a Type I error? Which will produce the smaller probability of a Type II error? Which significance level would you suggest be used? Explain your answer.

(e) What change would have to be made in the management's procedure in order to reduce the probability of a Type II error without affecting the probability of a Type I error?

(f) Consider the following two scenarios:
   (A)   The actual value of p is 0.002.
   (B)   The actual value of p is 0.008.

   For which of these two scenarios is a Type II error less likely?

(g) Suppose that the probability of a Type II error occurring when $p = 0.008$ is 0.07. What is the power of the test for that value of p? What is the meaning of power in this context?

9. NONLINEAR REGRESSION

9.1

Each year, a newspaper reports the daily circulation of its print version. The values for the years 2010 to 2016 are shown in the table below.

Year	Daily Circulation
2010	899900
2011	813000
2012	738700
2013	663300
2014	587200
2015	531800
2016	481200

First, a linear regression analysis was run for log(daily circulation) against years since 2000. (Here, "log" denotes log base 10.) Part of the computer output and a residual plot are shown below.

```
Predictor            Coef         SE Coef      T          P
Constant             6.41489      0.00772      831.45     0.000
Years since 2000     -0.0458562   0.0005866    -78.17     0.000

S = 0.00310391 R-Sq = 99.9% R-Sq(adj) = 99.9%
```

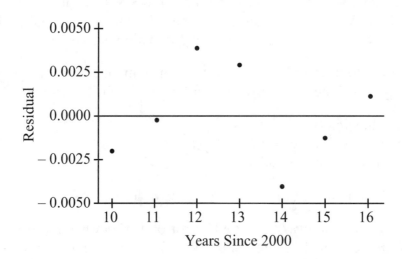

Second, a linear regression analysis was run for log(daily circulation) against log(years since 2000). Part of the computer output and a residual plot are shown below.

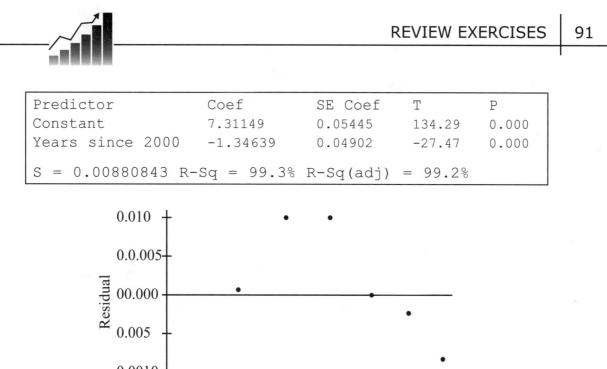

Predictor	Coef	SE Coef	T	P
Constant	7.31149	0.05445	134.29	0.000
Years since 2000	-1.34639	0.04902	-27.47	0.000

S = 0.00880843 R-Sq = 99.3% R-Sq(adj) = 99.2%

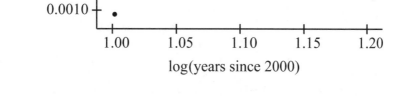

(a) Which of the two transformations above is more successful in producing a linear relationship? What is it about the residual plots that tells you this?

(b) For the transformation you chose in part (a), what is the equation of the least squares regression line relating log(daily circulation) to years since 2000 or log(daily circulation) to log(years since 2000)?

(c) What does your chosen model predict for the daily circulation of this newspaper in the year 2020? How much faith would you place in this estimate?

SAMPLE EXAMINATION ONE
SECTION I

Time—1 hour and 30 minutes
Number of questions—40
Percent of total grade—50

Directions: Solve each of the following problems, using the available space for scratch work. Decide which is the best of the choices given and fill in the corresponding oval on the answer sheet. No credit will be given for anything written in the test book. Do not spend too much time on any one problem.

1. A sample of 25 nine-year-olds was selected, and every child in the sample was observed for a day. The amounts of time (in minutes) these children spent using electronic devices that day are shown in the stemplot below. ("2|8" represents 28 minutes.)

```
1 | 9
2 | 8  9  0  9  6
3 | 4  1  4  9  8
4 | 5  4  1  5  7  6  3
5 | 0  1  4  8
6 | 0
7 |
8 | 2
9 | 9
```

Note that the leaves have not been placed in order in the stemplot. What is the median, in minutes, of the times spent using electronic devices?

(A) 42
(B) 43
(C) 44.5
(D) 45
(E) 50

Answer

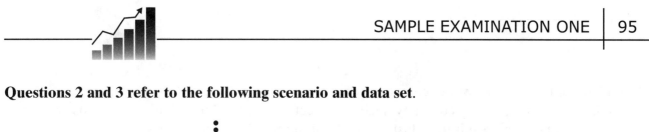

Questions 2 and 3 refer to the following scenario and data set.

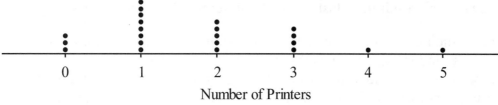

Number of Printers

In a class of 22 students, each student was asked how many printers there were in his or her home. (Fax machines were counted as printers, also.) The responses are shown in the dot plot below.

2. Which of the following is the interquartile range of this data set?

(A) 1   (B) 1.5   (C) 2   (D) 2.5   (E) 3

Answer

3. Which of the following best describes the shape of the distribution of the number of printers?

(A) Approximately normal
(B) Bimodal
(C) Negatively skewed
(D) Positively skewed
(E) Roughly symmetrical

Answer

4. A chain of large home improvement stores is conducting a review of its marketing strategy. As part of the review, the company needs to select a sample of the items that it sells. Which of the following will result in a cluster sample of items sold at one of its stores?

(A) Number the items sold at the store 1 through n, where n is the total number of items, and use a random number generator to select 200 of the items.

(B) Number the items sold at the store 1 through n, where n is the total number of items; the sample consists of the 20th item, the 40th item, the 60th item, and so on.

(C) Classify the items for sale at the store according to the categories "high priced," "medium-high priced," "medium-low priced," and "low priced." Randomly select 50 items from each category.

(D) Randomly select six departments in the store; the sample consists of all the items in the departments selected.

(E) Access computer records of the items bought by the first 20 customers on a particular day; these items form the sample.

Answer

5. Let A and B be two possible events when a random number generator is used once. Suppose you are told that A and B are mutually exclusive. This implies that

(A) the probability that A and B both happen is equal to the sum of the probabilities of A and B

(B) the probability that A and B both happen is equal to the product of the probabilities of A and B

(C) the probability that either A happens or B happens is equal to the sum of the probabilities of A and B

(D) the probability that either A happens or B happens is equal to the product of the probabilities of A and B

(E) the probability that A happens given that B happens is equal to the probability that A happens

Answer

6. In a culinary class of 15 students, each student is given a cut of meat. The cuts are of the same type of meat and are of similar size. The students are then asked to cut the meat into small sections known as "cubes." For each student, the teacher collects the cubes, counts them, and weighs them. For any given student, let x be the average weight of the cubes and let y be the number of cubes. If the values of x and y for all the students are plotted on a scatterplot, which of the following is most likely to be the result?

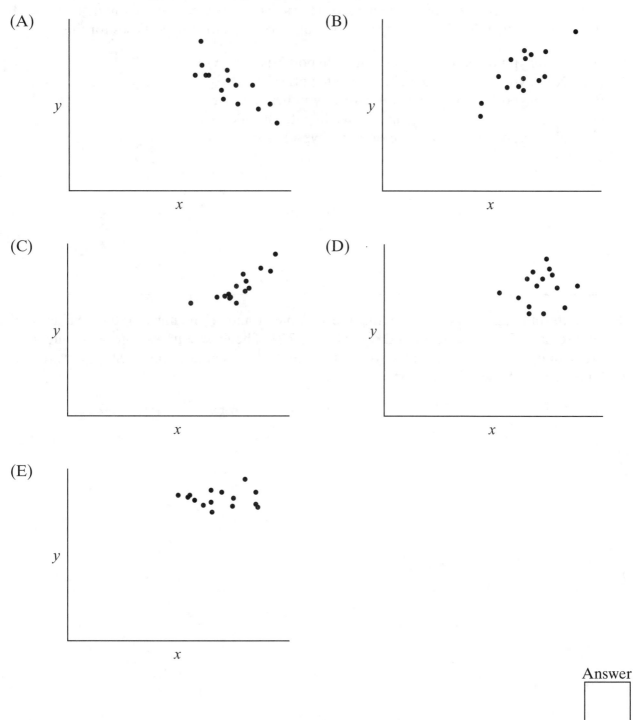

(A)

(B)

(C)

(D)

(E)

Answer

7. Students who wish to go to graduate school are often required to take a graduate record exam. It has been suggested that students who prepare using a paper prep book do better, on average, than students who use the online prep materials provided by the exam's administrators. In order to investigate this claim, the mean score, $\bar{x}_1$, for a random sample of students who use a paper prep book will be compared to the mean score, $\bar{x}_2$, for a random sample of students who use the online materials. Let the mean score for all students who use paper prep books be μ_1 and the mean score for all students who use the online materials be μ_2. Which of the following are appropriate null and alternative hypotheses for this study?

(A) Null hypothesis: $\bar{x}_1 = \bar{x}_2$; alternative hypothesis: $\bar{x}_1 > \bar{x}_2$
(B) Null hypothesis: $\bar{x}_1 = \bar{x}_2$; alternative hypothesis: $\bar{x}_1 \geq \bar{x}_2$
(C) Null hypothesis: $\bar{x}_1 > \bar{x}_2$; alternative hypothesis: $\bar{x}_1 = \bar{x}_2$
(D) Null hypothesis: $\mu_1 = \mu_2$; alternative hypothesis: $\mu_1 > \mu_2$
(E) Null hypothesis: $\mu_1 > \mu_2$; alternative hypothesis: $\mu_1 = \mu_2$

Answer

8. A scatterplot has been drawn relating the variables x and y. The mean of the x-values in the data set is 4.73 and the mean of the y-values is 7.21. The least squares regression line for predicting values of y from values of x has slope 0.482. What does the least squares regression line predict for the value of y when $x = 6.2$?

(A) 7.05   (B) 7.24   (C) 7.48   (D) 7.69   (E) 7.92

Answer

9. By definition, the mean intelligence quotient (IQ) for all children is 100. A study was conducted in the town of Wendleboro. A random sample of children was selected from the town, and the IQ of each child in the sample was found. These results were used to conduct a hypothesis test of $H_0: \mu = 100$ *versus* $H_a: \mu \neq 100$, where μ is the mean IQ for all children in Wendleboro. The *p*-value for the test was 0.243, which is larger than any commonly-used significance level. Which of the following is a correct conclusion to this hypothesis test?

   (A) The results provide convincing evidence that the mean IQ for all children in Wendleboro is equal to 100.
   (B) The results provide convincing evidence that the mean IQ for all children in Wendleboro is not equal to 100.
   (C) The results provide convincing evidence that the mean IQ for all children in Wendleboro is greater than 100.
   (D) The results do not provide convincing evidence that the mean IQ for all children in Wendleboro is equal to 100.
   (E) The results do not provide convincing evidence that the mean IQ for all children in Wendleboro is different from 100.

Answer

10. The manager of a large online computer users' group conducted a survey of participants using a random sample. Each person in the sample was asked whether his or her computer was backed-up regularly. Using the results of the survey a 95% confidence interval for the proportion, *p*, of all participants in the users' group whose computers were backed-up regularly was calculated to be $(0.135, 0.238)$. Which of the following is a correct interpretation of this interval?

   (A) If *p* were outside the interval $(0.135, 0.238)$ then a sample proportion as large or as small as the one in the study would be unlikely.
   (B) In repeated sampling, 95% of sample proportions would lie in the interval $(0.135, 0.238)$.
   (C) We are 95% confident that the proportion of people included in the sample whose computers are backed-up regularly is between 0.135 and 0.238.
   (D) 95% of all participants have computers that are backed-up less than a quarter of the time.
   (E) Since 0.2 is in the interval there is convincing evidence that *p* differs from 0.2.

Answer

Questions 11 and 12 refer to the following scenario.

A graduate student is comparing the effectiveness of two different approaches to learning, known as "repeated reading" and "multiple quizzing." With the cooperation of the teacher of a 6th-grade course she compiles a list of the 36 topics in the course. Using a computer, she randomly assigns a ten-digit decimal to each topic, and sorts the topics according to the random decimals. The students in the class then learn the first 18 topics on the resulting list using repeated reading and the other 18 topics using multiple quizzing. On the final exam, the performance of the students on the topics taught using repeated reading is compared to the students' performance on the topics taught using multiple quizzing.

11. Which of the following is true?

   (A) This is an observational study in which a stratified random sample of topics is used.
   (B) This is an observational study in which a simple random sample of topics is selected.
   (C) This is an experiment in which the students are randomly assigned to the treatments.
   (D) This is an experiment in which the two sets of topics form blocks according to learning approach.
   (E) This is an experiment with a completely randomized design.

Answer

12. Suppose that the person who grades the final exam does not know which topics were learned using which method. This is an example of

   (A) blinding
   (B) direct control
   (C) a placebo
   (D) randomization
   (E) replication

Answer

13. Which of the following is/are true?

      I. Some t distributions are negatively skewed.
     II. Some chi-square distributions are negatively skewed.
    III. Some binomial distributions are negatively skewed.

(A) II only
(B) III only
(C) I and II
(D) I and III
(E) None of the statements is true.

Answer

14. The administration of a large university has been encouraging students to set aside money for future needs. In order to investigate the success of the campaign, a random sample of 100 students was selected. Each student in the sample was asked to state, privately, how much money he or she had saved for future needs. Using the sample values, a hypothesis test was conducted concerning the population mean amount saved. Using a sample size that was greater than 30 ensured that

(A) the distribution of the amounts saved for all the students at the university was approximately normal
(B) the distribution of the amounts saved for the students in the sample was approximately normal
(C) the distribution of all possible sample mean amounts saved was approximately normal
(D) the standard deviation of the amounts saved in the population was small
(E) the standard deviation of the amounts saved in the sample was small

15. As part of an online course on character education, participants are required to take a survey that measures their character strengths. A researcher, using the results for participants who had already taken the course, made a scatterplot using the variables x = amount of zest and y = amount of love of learning. (Zest means energy and enthusiasm.) A computer was used to find the equation of the least squares regression line for predicting love of learning from zest, and the value of the coefficient of determination, r^2, was found to be 0.68. Which of the following best explains this value?

(A) 68% of the variation in love of learning is accounted for by the least squares regression line

(B) 68% of the variation in zest is accounted for by the least squares regression line

(C) 68% of the relationship between zest and love of learning is accounted for by the least squares regression line

(D) 68% of people who have zest also love learning

(E) 68% of people who love learning also have zest

Answer

16. A large company conducted a study of email use by its employees. In a random sample of 212 messages sent by males, 18 contained emoticons, and in an independent random sample of 186 messages sent by females, 26 contained emoticons. (An emoticon is a facial expression created in the message, often using punctuation marks.) A hypothesis test was conducted with a 5% significance level to determine whether these results provided convincing evidence that the proportion of messages sent by female employees that contain emoticons is greater than the equivalent proportion for male employees. Denoting the p-value for the test by p, which of the following is true?

(A) $p > 0.05$; there is convincing evidence of a greater proportion of female messages containing emoticons than male messages

(B) $p > 0.05$; there is not convincing evidence of a greater proportion of female messages containing emoticons than male messages

(C) $0.01 < p < 0.05$; there is convincing evidence of a greater proportion of female messages containing emoticons than male messages

(D) $0.01 < p < 0.05$; there is not convincing evidence of a greater proportion of female messages containing emoticons than male messages

(E) $p < 0.01$; there is not convincing evidence of a greater proportion of female messages containing emoticons than male messages

Answer

17. Einstein claimed that imagination is more important than knowledge. However, recent psychological studies have brought evidence against this claim. In order to investigate the opinions of professional educators, a random sample of high school teachers will be selected. Each teacher in the sample will be asked whether he or she agrees with the statement,

"Knowledge is every bit as important as imagination."

The sample proportion of teachers, $\hat{p}$, who agree with the statement will be used to estimate the proportion of all high school teachers who agree with the statement, and a confidence interval will be constructed.

Assume that the sample size and confidence level are fixed. Which of the following sample proportions

$$\hat{p} = 0.1, \hat{p} = 0.5, \hat{p} = 0.9,$$

will produce the greatest margin of error for the estimate of the population proportion?

(A) $\hat{p} = 0.1$, only
(B) $\hat{p} = 0.5$, only
(C) $\hat{p} = 0.9$, only
(D) $\hat{p} = 0.1$ and $\hat{p} = 0.9$
(E) The margin of error is not dependent on the value of $\hat{p}$.

Answer

18. E-Z pass is an electronic toll-collection system used in many US states. Suppose that 18% of vehicles that pass through an E-Z pass lane are trucks. Given that the types of vehicles occur independently of each other, what is the probability that less than 3 of the next 8 vehicles passing through this lane are trucks?

(A)   0.040
(B)   0.121
(C)   0.635
(D)   0.839
(E)   0.960

Answer

19. By checking online at her phone provider's website, Samantha can see the lengths of calls she has made. The calls are listed in whole numbers of minutes. Samantha lists the lengths of all the calls she made on a particular day. These call lengths are shown in the histogram below.

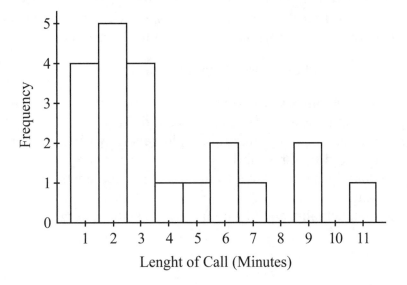

For a call selected at random from those made that day, what is the probability that the listed length of the call was 5 minutes or less, given that it was not 1 minute?

(A) 0.524   (B) 0.578   (C) 0.647   (D) 0.714   (E) 0.882

Answer

20. A particular state has recently introduced a law that includes possible prison sentences for distracted driving. In order to investigate the reaction of adults who live in the state, the public opinion department of a magazine sent a questionnaire to a random sample of 200 state residents. Eighty-two people responded to the survey, and their answers, generally speaking, showed approval for the law. This result was used in the magazine to describe the opinions of adults in the state as a whole with regard to the new law.

Which of the following describes a possible bias in the study?

(A) The sample of 200 adults was too small.

(B) People vary a lot in their attitudes to distracted driving.

(C) Adults who respond to surveys like this might generally have opinions that differ from those of adults who do not respond.

(D) The sample could, by chance, have included many people who feel strongly about distracted driving.

(E) It is possible that, actually, adults who live in the state generally disapprove of the new law.

Answer

21. Five cumulative relative frequency graphs are shown below. A statistician decides to compare the variability of the five distributions, using

$$(70\text{th percentile}) - (30\text{th percentile})$$

as the measure of variability.

By this measure, which has the largest variability?

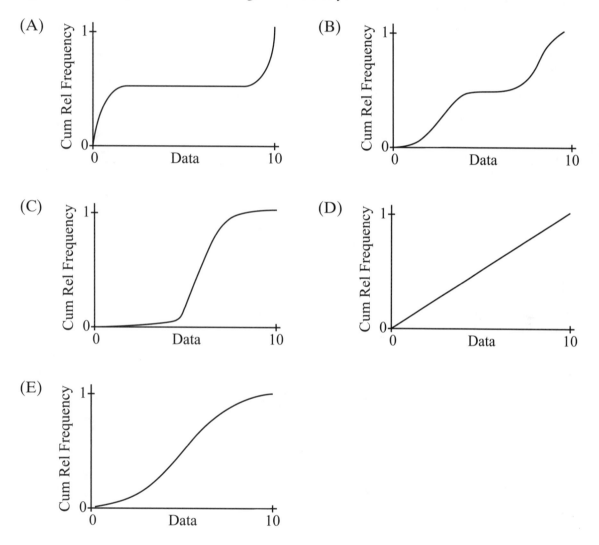

Answer

22. A farmer has Buff Orpington and Black Star chickens. He will select a random sample of n_1 eggs produced by Buff Orpingtons and an independent random sample of n_2 eggs produced by Black Stars. He will then weigh each of the eggs selected. He will denote the sample mean and sample standard deviation for the first sample by $\bar{x}_1$ and s_1, respectively, and the equivalent quantities for the second sample by $\bar{x}_2$ and s_2. The farmer wishes to find out whether the results of his samples provide convincing evidence of a difference between the population mean weights of eggs for the two breeds. Which of the following should be used as the standardized test statistic?

(A) $\dfrac{\bar{x}_1 - \bar{x}_2}{\sqrt{\dfrac{s_1}{n_1} + \dfrac{s_2}{n_2}}}$

(B) $\dfrac{\bar{x}_1 - \bar{x}_2}{\sqrt{\left(\dfrac{s_1 + s_2}{2}\right)\left(\dfrac{1}{n_1} + \dfrac{1}{n_2}\right)}}$

(C) $\dfrac{\bar{x}_1 - \bar{x}_2}{\sqrt{\dfrac{s_1^2}{n_1} + \dfrac{s_2^2}{n_2}}}$

(D) $\dfrac{\bar{x}_1 - \bar{x}_2}{\left(\dfrac{s_1}{n_1} + \dfrac{s_2}{n_2}\right)}$

(E) $\dfrac{\bar{x}_1 - \bar{x}_2}{\left(\dfrac{s_1^2}{n_1} + \dfrac{s_2^2}{n_2}\right)}$

Answer

23. For several years, a political party has had 38% support among the population of potential voters. However, the party has recently changed its branding, and the party leadership wishes to know whether support for the party has changed. A random sample of voters is selected, and each person in the sample is asked whether he or she supports the party. Using the results, a hypothesis test is performed in order to find out whether there is convincing evidence of a change in the level of support for the party. A standardized z statistic is used, and a p-value is calculated. The p-value is

(A) the probability that support for the party has not changed
(B) the probability that support for the party has changed
(C) the probability of getting the z statistic calculated in the study, given that support for the party has not changed
(D) the probability of getting a z statistic at least as far above zero as the one in the study, given that support for the party has not changed
(E) the probability of getting a z statistic at least as far from zero as the one in the study, given that support for the party has not changed

Answer

24. Monty the Mouse is given two doors to choose from, and he must choose one of the doors. Behind one of the doors there is a small piece of goat cheese; behind the other door there is nothing. Suppose that Monty goes through the same procedure every day for a sequence of 50 days. On each day the probability that Monty gets the cheese is equal to the probability that he does not get the cheese, and the outcome is independent of the outcomes on all the previous days. Let k be the probability that the proportion of days on which Monty gets the cheese is less than 0.53. Which of the following is closest to k?

(A) 0.664   (B) 0.684   (C) 0.704   (D) 0.724   (E) 0.744

Answer

25. An environmental health officer has been asked about levels of radon (a radioactive gas) in homes in a particular county. As an initial step to forming a response to this inquiry, the officer plans to randomly select 20 homes in the county. The level of radon in each of the 20 homes will be measured, and the sample mean, $\bar{x}$, and the sample standard deviation, s, will be calculated. Using these values, a 90% confidence interval will be constructed for the mean radon level for all homes in the county. The formula

$$\bar{x} \pm t^* \cdot \frac{s}{\sqrt{n}}$$

will be used for the confidence interval. Which of the following is the correct value of t^*?

(A) 1.325
(B) 1.328
(C) 1.645
(D) 1.725
(E) 1.729

Answer

26. A set of volunteers was gathered for a study. For each volunteer a coin was flipped. If the coin landed "heads" the volunteer was asked to eat a meal using a knife and fork; if the coin landed "tails" the volunteer was asked to eat a meal using a fork only. (All the meals were identical.) The mean time to eat the meal for those who used a knife and fork will be compared to the mean time for those who used a fork only. Assuming that the conditions for inference are met, which of the following could be used to make this comparison?

(A) Chi-square test for goodness of fit
(B) Two-sample t test
(C) Paired t test
(D) Two-sample z test for a difference in population proportions
(E) No hypothesis test is suitable, since the study did not use a random sample of people.

Answer

27. There were six manned moon landings, taking place between 1969 and 1972. A website lists, for each landing, the EVA time in hours. (EVA stands for *extravehicular activity*; EVA time in this context is time spent outside the spacecraft on the moon's surface.) The standard deviation of the six EVA times is 7.94 hours. The z-score for the EVA time for the first landing is -1.37 and the z-score for the EVA time for the last landing is 1.09. What is the difference, in hours, between the EVA times for these two landings?

(A) 2.22
(B) 3.23
(C) 4.98
(D) 19.53
(E) 28.36

Answer

28. A tourist is about to return a car to a car rental agency. Unfortunately, the car has suffered a minor scratch and the tourist is returning the car slightly late. Suppose that the probability that the tourist will be charged for the scratch is 0.2, the probability that he will be charged for returning the car late is 0.6, and that these two events are independent. What is the probability that the tourist will be charged for exactly one of these two things?

(A) 0.12   (B) 0.56   (C) 0.68   (D) 0.80   (E) 0.88

Answer

29. A random sample of size n will be taken from a large population of people. The weights of the n people in the sample will be measured. Let the sample standard deviation be s, and let the standard deviation of the sampling distribution of the sample mean be $\sigma_{\overline{X}}$. Consequently, the sample variance is s^2 and the variance of the sampling distribution of the sample mean is $\sigma_{\overline{X}}^2$. As n increases

(A) s^2 tends to increase and $\sigma_{\overline{X}}^2$ increases

(B) s^2 tends to increase and $\sigma_{\overline{X}}^2$ decreases

(C) s^2 tends to decrease and $\sigma_{\overline{X}}^2$ increases

(D) s^2 tends to decrease and $\sigma_{\overline{X}}^2$ decreases

(E) s^2 neither tends to increase nor tends to decrease, and $\sigma_{\overline{X}}^2$ decreases

Answer

30. A company is in the process of developing a machine to produce screws. The screws will be rejected if they are less than 12.0 millimeters or greater than 12.5 millimeters in diameter. Currently, the machine is producing screws whose diameters are normally distributed with mean 12.3 millimeters and standard deviation 0.2 millimeters. Let Z be the random variable with the standard normal distribution (the normal distribution with mean 0 and standard deviation 1). If the machine continues to run as it is currently, which of the following is the proportion of screws that will be rejected?

(A) $P(Z < 1) + P(Z < -1.5)$

(B) $P(Z < 1) - P(Z < -1.5)$

(C) $P(Z < -1.5) - P(Z < 1)$

(D) $1 - P(Z < -1.5) + P(Z < 1)$

(E) $1 - P(Z < 1) + P(Z < -1.5)$

Answer

31. An experiment is being designed to find out whether physical warmth increases feelings of interpersonal warmth (warmth toward a fellow human being). A researcher will speak to people in the street. If a person agrees to take part, the researcher will give the person a cup of coffee to hold while he (the researcher) sorts his papers. Using random assignment, for some participants the coffee will be warm and for the remaining participants the coffee will be iced. The researcher will then read a brief story to the participant, and, once the story is over, the participant will be asked whether he or she likes the main person in the story. The responses for those who held a cup of warm coffee will be compared to the responses of those who held a cup of iced coffee.

Which of the following is an example of confounding?

(A) People on the street are not necessarily representative of people in general.
(B) People are not all the same in their reactions to stories.
(C) At some times during the experiment it will be sunnier than at other times, and people respond more positively when it's sunny.
(D) The temperature of the coffee might affect the way the researcher reads the story.
(E) The main person in the story suffers some misfortunes, and this will make people sympathetic to the character.

Answer

32. In Springfield County, the median property tax last year was \$2,132 and the interquartile range of the property taxes was \$1,936. This year the property tax will first be increased by 8%, and then an additional amount of \$300 will be added for each home. This means that, for any given home, if x is last year's property tax, then this year's property tax will be $1.08x + 300$. Assume that there will be no new homes in Springfield County this year, and no homes will be removed. Which of the following shows the correct median and interquartile range of property taxes for this year (to the nearest dollar)?

(A) median = 2303, IQR = 1936
(B) median = 2303, IQR = 2091
(C) median = 2603, IQR = 1936
(D) median = 2603, IQR = 2091
(E) median = 2603, IQR = 2391

Answer

33. Roy has data based on independent random samples drawn from two populations. The sample sizes are $n_1 = 15$ and $n_2 = 12$. He plans to construct a two-sample t interval for the difference in the population means. He will draw a pair of boxplots (showing outliers) in order to check the conditions for inference. Which of the following pairs of boxplots would indicate that it is appropriate for Roy to proceed with construction of the confidence interval?

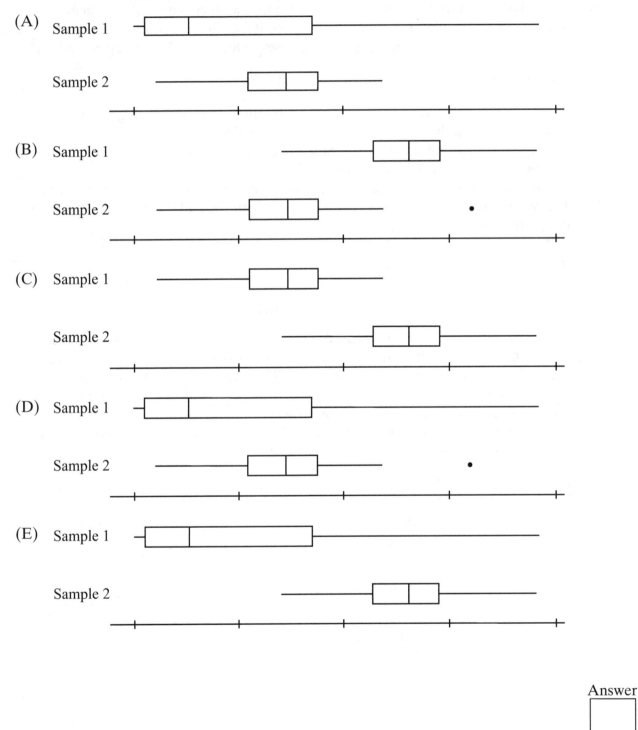

(A) Sample 1

Sample 2

(B) Sample 1

Sample 2

(C) Sample 1

Sample 2

(D) Sample 1

Sample 2

(E) Sample 1

Sample 2

Answer

34. Five students are discussing how long they studied for a quiz. They make a list of the 5 study times in minutes. The deviations from the mean, $x - \bar{x}$, for this data set are shown below.

$$-2.6 \quad -6.6 \quad 13.4 \quad 17.4 \quad -21.6$$

What is the sample standard deviation for the set of study times?

(A) 12.32 (B) 14.14 (C) 15.81 (D) 199.84 (E) 249.80

Answer

35. A random sample will be selected from a population of people, and each person in the sample will be asked a survey question. Using the proportion of people in the sample who answer "yes" to the question, a significance test will be performed using the hypotheses $H_0: p = 0.8$ versus $H_a: p < 0.8$, where p is the proportion of people in the population who would answer "yes" to the question. Which of the following best defines a Type II error in this context?

(A) Getting a sample proportion greater than 0.8 when $p < 0.8$
(B) Getting a sample proportion less than 0.8 when $p \geq 0.8$
(C) Getting a sample proportion that is small enough to reject H_0 when $p \geq 0.8$
(D) Getting a sample proportion that is <u>not</u> small enough to reject H_0 when $p < 0.8$
(E) Getting a sample proportion that is <u>not</u> small enough to reject H_0 when $p > 0.8$

Answer

36. Jake is using a table of random digits. He will start at a random point in the table, and then will move to the right along that line; when he reaches the end of a line, he will continue at the beginning of the next line. For which of the following is the random variable X geometrically distributed?

    (A) Note the first 10 digits; X is the number of eights noted.
    (B) Note each digit up to and including the first 0; X is the number of digits noted.
    (C) X is the value of the first digit encountered that is not 0.
    (D) Note each digit, but ignore any zeroes, sevens, eights, and nines; X is the sum of the first 10 digits noted.
    (E) Take two digits at a time; note the first 10 two-digit numbers encountered, but ignoring repeats; X is the number of two-digit numbers noted that are less than 33

Answer

37. A random sample will be selected from a population, and a hypothesis test will be performed using the hypotheses $H_0: \mu = 10$ *versus* $H_a: \mu > 10$, where μ is the population mean. It is known that the power of the test when $\mu = 11$ is 0.78. Which of the following is a correct interpretation of this statement?

    (A) If H_0 is true, the probability that H_0 will not be rejected is 0.78.
    (B) If H_a is true, we are 78% confident that $\mu = 11$.
    (C) If $\mu = 11$, the probability that H_0 will be rejected is 0.78.
    (D) In repeated sampling, 78% of the time we will get convincing evidence that $\mu > 11$.
    (E) The probability of getting a sample mean of at least 11 when H_0 is true is 0.78.

Answer

38. When Emma types "RandInt(1,8)" into her calculator and presses "Enter", the outcome is a random integer between 1 and 8 inclusive. The standard deviation of the outcome when this function is accessed is 2.291. Emma will access the function four times (producing four independent outcomes), and will add the four outcomes, calling her total S. Emma's friend, Josie, will access the function once and will multiply the outcome by 4, calling her result T. Which of the following is true about the standard deviations of the random variables S and T?

(A) $\sigma_S = 2.291, \sigma_T = 2.291$

(B) $\sigma_S = 4.582, \sigma_T = 9.164$

(C) $\sigma_S = 9.164, \sigma_T = 4.582$

(D) $\sigma_S = 9.164, \sigma_T = 9.164$

(E) $\sigma_S = 9.164, \sigma_T = 36.656$

Answer

39. An experiment was conducted using college students. Each participant was given an empty soda can in a room that contained a recycling bin and a trash receptacle. Using random assignment, for some of the participants the can had simply been emptied of soda, and for others the can had been both emptied and squashed. Each participant was then asked to dispose of the can, and the researchers observed whether the student placed the can in the recycling bin or in the trash receptacle. It was found that the proportion of students with non-squashed soda cans who recycled the can, $\hat{p}_1$, was 0.13 greater than the equivalent proportion, $\hat{p}_2$, for students with cans that were squashed. On the basis of this result the study found convincing evidence that a student is more likely to recycle a can if it is not squashed. Which of the following was the rationale behind this conclusion?

(A) If students are equally likely to recycle non-squashed cans as they are to recycle squashed cans, then the study would be very unlikely to produce an experimental result of $\hat{p}_1 - \hat{p}_2 \geq 0.13$.

(B) If students are equally likely to recycle non-squashed cans as they are to recycle squashed cans, then the study would be very unlikely to produce an experimental result of $\hat{p}_1 - \hat{p}_2 < 0.13$.

(C) If students are more likely to recycle non-squashed cans than squashed cans, then the study would be likely to produce an experimental result of $\hat{p}_1 - \hat{p}_2 = 0.13$.

(D) If students are more likely to recycle non-squashed cans than squashed cans, then the study would be likely to produce an experimental result of $\hat{p}_1 - \hat{p}_2 \geq 0.13$.

(E) If the probability that a student will recycle a non-squashed can is 0.13 greater than the equivalent probability for a squashed can, then the study would be likely to produce an experimental result of $\hat{p}_1 - \hat{p}_2 = 0.13$.

Answer

40. A country is reviewing its military recruitment policy. As part of the review, a random sample of adults is selected from the country. Each person in the sample is asked whether he or she agrees with the statement,

"It is acceptable for women to engage in active military service."

Additionally, the gender of each respondent is noted. The results are shown in the table below.

Observed

	Agree	Disagree
Male	177	330
Female	193	289

A chi-square test is performed to determine whether there is convincing evidence of an association between response and gender. The expected counts are shown in the table below.

Expected

	Agree	Disagree
Male	177	330
Female	193	289

Using the observed and expected counts as shown, the value of the chi-square (χ^2) statistic is calculated. This value is compared to the chi-square critical value appropriate to this test for a 5% significance level. Which of the following is true?

(A) $\chi^2 = 2.779$, which is less than the critical value

(B) $\chi^2 = 2.779$, which is greater than the critical value

(C) $\chi^2 = 2.785$, which is less than the critical value

(D) $\chi^2 = 2.785$, which is greater than the critical value

(E) $\chi^2 = 2.693$, which is less than the critical value

Answer

SECTION II PART A

Questions 1–5
Spend about 65 minutes on this part of the exam.
Percent of Section II grade—75

Directions: Show all your work. Indicate clearly the methods you use, because you will be graded on the correctness of your method as well as on the accuracy and completeness of your results and explanations.

1. The populations (in millions) of the 50 states (and the District of Columbia) were estimated in 2014. The results are summarized in the table below.

populations $< Q_1$	Q_1	Median	Q_3	populations $> Q_3$
0.6, 0.6, 0.7, 0.7, 0.7, 0.9, 0.9, 1.0, 1.1, 1.3, 1.3, 1.4	1.6	4.4	7.0	8.3, 8.9, 9.9, 9.9, 10.1, 11.6, 12.8, 12.9, 19.7, 19.9, 27.0, 38.8

(a) Which values in the data set are outliers? Show how you arrive at your answer.

(b)   Using the axis given below, construct a boxplot that shows the outliers.

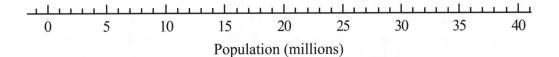

Population (millions)

(c)   At the time of the study, the estimated population of Missouri was 6.1 million. To what extent, in terms of population, could Missouri be described as a "large state"?

2. A stallholder is offering a game at a local charity fair. The stallholder has two spinners, as shown in the diagram below. (The six outcomes on Spinner 1 are equally likely, and the four outcomes on Spinner 2 are equally likely.)

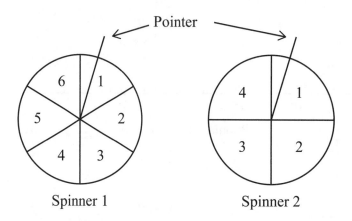

For each participant, the stallholder spins the pointers on both spinners. The participant wins an amount in dollars given by the <u>difference</u> of the two scores. (For example, if Spinner 1's pointer stops on 6 and Spinner 2's pointer stops on 2, then the participant wins $6 - 2 = 4$ dollars. If Spinner 1's pointer stops on 1 and Spinner 2's pointer stops on 4, then the participant wins $4 - 1 = 3$ dollars.)

(a)   Complete the table below by writing in each cell the amount won by the participant.

		Score on Spinner 1					
		1	2	3	4	5	6
Score on Spinner 2	1						
	2						4
	3						
	4	3					

(b) Complete the table below, giving the probability distribution of the amount in dollars won by the participant.

Amount Won ($)	0	1	2	3	4	5
Probability						

(c) The expected value of the amount won by the participant is $1.83. Explain how this value is calculated.

(d) The stallholder charges $2.50 for each play of the game. How much money can the stallholder expect to make for the charity on a day when there are 400 plays of the game?

3. The healthcare research agency of a large state decides to investigate how expensive healthcare is at the state's hospitals. A statistician working for the agency is asked to select a sample of hospitals from the 439 hospitals in the state.

(a) Suppose that the statistician has a computer list of all 439 hospitals. How might she use the computer to select a simple random sample of 40 hospitals?

The statistician now considers a different approach. She will use a stratified random sample, with the following four strata:

(1) urban teaching hospitals
(2) urban non-teaching hospitals
(3) rural teaching hospitals
(4) rural non-teaching hospitals

(Note: A teaching hospital is a hospital that is affiliated with a medical school; students at the medical school receive training at the hospital.)

(b) Explain how a stratified random sample of 40 hospitals might be selected, using the strata described above.

(c)   Explain why "urban/rural" and "teaching status" might be considered suitable stratification variables.

4. A team of educational psychologists performed an experiment using a class of 12 elementary school students. The students were randomly assigned to two groups of six students each, Group A and Group B. The students in Group A were given an activity lasting 30 minutes, and the students' on-task times were recorded. (A student is said to be "on task" if he or she is engaging in the assigned activity.) On a second occasion, the students in Group A were given a very similar 30-minute activity, but this time classical music was playing in the room. The students in Group B were given the same treatments, except that for these students there was classical music playing on the first occasion, and no music on the second occasion. The results for all 12 students are shown below.

Student	1	2	3	4	5	6	7	8	9	10	11	12
No Music	26	10	19	25	8	23	21	13	9	26	10	25
Music	27	7	20	28	5	24	24	12	11	26	12	24

Do these results provide convincing evidence that, for students like the ones in this study, the true mean on-task time when music is playing is greater than when there is no music? Provide statistical justification for your answer.

5. A beaker of pure water was heated to a number of different temperatures, ranging from 0°C to 50°C. At each temperature, the pH of the water was measured. (Note: pH is a measure of acidity. A pH of 7 is neutral, and values below 7 indicate acidity.) Part of the regression analysis for predicting pH based on temperature is shown below.

```
Predictor      Coef        SE Coef     T        P
Constant       7.418       0.111       66.74    0.000
Temperature    -0.01670    0.00376     -4.44    0.007

S = 0.157181   R-Sq = 79.80%   R-Sq(adj) = 75.76%
```

(a) Use the computer output above to determine the equation of the least squares regression line. Identify any variables used in your equation.

(b) When the water was heated to a temperature of 30°C the pH was 7.08. Calculate the residual for this observation, and explain the meaning of this residual in the context of this study.

(c) Does the information in the computer output provide convincing evidence of a linear relationship between temperature and pH? Explain your answer.

SECTION II PART B

Question 6
Spend about 25 minutes on this part of the exam.
Percent of Section II grade—25

Directions: Show all your work. Indicate clearly the methods you use, because you will be graded on the correctness of your method as well as on the accuracy and completeness of your results and explanations.

6. A student named Emily has a number cube with faces numbered 1 through 6. When the cube is rolled, the six outcomes are equally likely. Let the score for a single roll of this cube be X.

(a) Suppose that the number cube will be rolled n times and the mean, $\overline{X}$, of the n scores will be calculated. What does the Central Limit Theorem tell you about the distribution of $\overline{X}$?

Emily's class is asked to investigate the distribution of the mean score, $\overline{X}$, for 10 rolls of the number cube ($n = 10$). Emily rolls the number cube 10 times, and gets the scores shown below.

$$5 \quad 3 \quad 4 \quad 6 \quad 1 \quad 3 \quad 4 \quad 3 \quad 6 \quad 1$$

(b) What is the value of $\overline{X}$ for this sequence of 10 rolls?

128

The other students in Emily's class have number cubes that are the same as Emily's. Together they generate 100 different values of $\overline{X}$. (This involves performing 100 sets of 10 rolls of the number cubes.) The values of $\overline{X}$ they obtain are summarized by the observed counts in the table below.

$\overline{X}$	≤ 3.15	3.15–3.45	3.45–3.75	3.75–4.05	≥ 4.05
Observed Count	20	20	28	21	11

(c) The expected value and the standard deviation of the score, X, when one number cube is rolled are known to be 3.5 and 1.708, respectively. From these values, the expected value and the standard deviation of the sampling distribution of the mean score, $\overline{X}$, for a sequence of 10 rolls of the cube are calculated to be 3.5 and 0.540, respectively. Explain how the value 0.540 is calculated.

The students in the class are asked to investigate whether the observed counts in the table approximately fit a normal distribution.

(d) If $\overline{X}$ actually was normally distributed with mean 3.5 and standard deviation 0.540, how many of the 100 values of $\overline{X}$ would you expect to be less than or equal to 3.15? Show the calculations that lead to your answer.

The expected counts for three of the categories (assuming that $\overline{X}$ is normally distributed with mean 3.5 and standard deviation 0.540) are shown in the table below.

$\overline{X}$	≤ 3.15	3.15–3.45	3.45–3.75	3.75–4.05	≥ 4.05
Observed Count	20	20	28	21	11
Expected Count			21.52	16.75	15.42

(e)

   i. At the appropriate place in the table, write the expected count you calculated in part (d).

  ii. The table should now show four of the five expected counts. By subtracting these four expected counts from 100, calculate the remaining expected count, and write this value at the appropriate place in the table.

Using the numbers in the table above, Emily analyzes the results of the class's investigation by performing a chi-square goodness of fit test. She uses the hypotheses

H_0: the sampling distribution of $\overline{X}$ is exactly normal

versus

H_a: the sampling distribution of $\overline{X}$ is not exactly normal.

(f) The *p*-value for this hypothesis test is 0.229. In the context of the class's investigation, what should be the conclusion to the test?

(g) Does the conclusion in part (f) involve a Type I error, a Type II error, or neither? Explain your answer.

SAMPLE EXAMINATION TWO
SECTION I

Time—1 hour and 30 minutes
Number of questions—40
Percent of total grade—50

Directions: Solve each of the following problems, using the available space for scratch work. Decide which is the best of the choices given and fill in the corresponding oval on the answer sheet. No credit will be given for anything written in the test book. Do not spend too much time on any one problem.

1. Drivers taking a mandated driving safety course are given a quiz at the end of an evening lecture. The scores are summarized in the boxplot below.

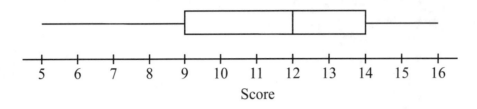

Score

In order to motivate the participants, the instructor adds two points to each student's score. Which of the following is <u>not</u> true about the resulting data set?

(A) Minimum = 7
(B) Median = 14
(C) Upper quartile = 16
(D) Maximum = 18
(E) Interquartile range = 7

Answer

2. Downtown Music sells CDs. Currently, 83 percent of the CDs in the store are classical, 63 percent are used, and 51 percent are used classical CDs. Tomorrow a sale will be begin, and the sale will include those CDs that are either classical or used (or both). No other CDs will be included in the sale. What percentage of the store's CDs will be included in the sale?

(A) 95   (B) 93   (C) 91   (D) 88   (E) 71

Answer

3. Natalie is a statistics student at a large high school. She has designed a questionnaire that is intended to discover whether or not the respondent is a procrastinator. Natalie selects a random sample of 48 students from the school, and each student in the sample agrees to answer the questions in the questionnaire. Having analyzed the responses, Natalie discovers that, according to her definition, 29 of the students in the sample are procrastinators. At what significance level does Natalie have convincing evidence that more than half of the students at the school are procrastinators?

(A)   At the 1%, 5% and 10% levels
(B)   At the 1% and 5% levels, but not at the 10% level
(C)   At the 5%, and 10% levels but not at the 1% level
(D)   At the 1% level, but not at the 5% or 10% levels
(E)   At the 10% level but not at the 1% or 5% levels

Answer

Questions 4 and 5 refer to the following scenario.

A pharmaceutical company is setting up an experiment to test a drug designed to reduce the symptoms of depression. Patients who suffer from depression will be asked to volunteer, and the participants will be randomly assigned to two groups: Group A and Group B. The patients in Group A will be given the drug in the form of tablets, while the patients in Group B will be given tablets that appear identical to the drug, but in fact contain no active ingredient. The progress of all the patients will then be monitored.

4. The Group B patients will be given tablets rather than nothing at all so that

   (A) the effects of the drug on the patients in Group A can be disregarded
   (B) both groups experience the psychological effect of being given a treatment
   (C) both groups receive some sort of drug
   (D) only the patients in Group A experience the side effects of the drug
   (E) no participant experiences the placebo effect

Answer

5. Originally, finances were made available for only 10 participants in the experiment, so that there would be 5 participants in each group. However, a statistician involved in the experimental design has asked that a greater number of participants be used. The main reason for including a larger number of participants is that, with a larger number of participants

   (A) the people who are given the drug are likely to experience a larger effect, while the people who are not given the drug will respond in roughly the same way
   (B) the people who are given the drug are likely to experience a larger effect, while the people who are not given the drug are likely to experience a smaller effect
   (C) the variability in the results within any one of the two groups is likely to be smaller
   (D) chance differences between the two groups in terms of the people included are likely to be smaller
   (E) for the people who are not given the drug, the psychological effect of being given a treatment will be greater

Answer

6. A survey was conducted in order to find out whether there is any difference between the happiness experienced by high-income versus low-income adults. A random sample of 152 high-income adults and an independent random sample of 212 low-income adults were selected. The people selected were given survey questions, and, using their answers, a "happiness score" out of 50 was calculated for each person. A hypothesis test was conducted, and the computer output for the hypothesis test is shown below.

```
Two-sample T for HighIncome vs LowIncome

             N      Mean     StDev     SE Mean
HighIncome  152     35.33    5.07      0.41
LowIncome   212     34.45    5.08      0.35

S = 5418.57     R-Sq = 25.8%     R-Sq(adj) = 18.4%

Difference = μ (HighIncome) - μ (LowIncome)
Estimate for difference:  0.878
95% CI for difference:  (-0.184, 1.939)
T-Test of difference = 0 (vs ≠): T-Value = 1.63
P-Value = 0.105  DF = 325
```

A 5% level of significance will be used for the hypothesis test. Which of the following is a correct conclusion to the study?

(A) There is convincing evidence that high-income adults are, on average, happier than low-income adults.

(B) There is convincing evidence that low-income adults are, on average, happier than high-income adults.

(C) There is convincing evidence that the average happiness for high-income adults is equal to the average happiness for low-income adults.

(D) There is not convincing evidence that the average happiness for high-income adults differs from the average happiness for low-income adults.

(E) Low-income adults in the study on average showed a higher level of happiness than the high-income adults in the study.

Answer

7. Derek works for a car rental company. The company currently owns 1,744 cars, and the cars are sorted into size categories (compact, standard, full size, premium, and SUV). Additionally, the company has a record, for each car, of its current value in dollars, calculated according to the car's model, exact age, and mileage. Derek has been asked to prepare two graphs. The first graph should show the number of cars in each size category, and the second graph should show the distribution of the current values for the 1,744 cars. Suppose that, for each graph, Derek will choose between a bar chart and a histogram. Which of the following is the best choice?

(A) Both graphs should be bar charts.
(B) Both graphs should be histograms.
(C) The size category graph should be a bar chart and the value graph should be a histogram.
(D) The size category graph should be a histogram and the value graph should be a bar chart.
(E) Neither a histogram nor a bar chart is suitable for the size category data.

Answer

8. A survey was conducted using independent random samples of 385 professional scientists and 622 members of the general public. It was found that 339 of the scientists and 317 of the members of the public believed that climate change is mostly caused by human activity.

Note that $339/385 = 0.881$, $317/622 = 0.510$, and $(339 + 317)/(385 + 622) = 0.651$.

Which of the following represents a 90% confidence interval for the difference between the proportion of all scientists and the proportion of all members of the public who believe that climate change is mostly caused by human activity?

(A) $(0.881 - 0.510) \pm 1.282 \sqrt{\dfrac{(0.881)(0.119)}{385} + \dfrac{(0.510)(0.490)}{622}}$

(B) $(0.881 - 0.510) \pm 1.645 \sqrt{\dfrac{(0.881)(0.119)}{385} + \dfrac{(0.510)(0.490)}{622}}$

(C) $(0.881 - 0.510) \pm 1.282 \sqrt{\dfrac{(0.651)(0.349)}{385} + \dfrac{(0.651)(0.349)}{622}}$

(D) $(0.881 - 0.510) \pm 1.645 \sqrt{\dfrac{(0.651)(0.349)}{385} + \dfrac{(0.651)(0.349)}{622}}$

(E) $0.651 \pm 1.645 \sqrt{\dfrac{(0.651)(0.349)}{385} + \dfrac{(0.651)(0.349)}{622}}$

Answer

9. The owners of a large shopping mall wish to estimate the proportion of shoppers at the mall who are female. They will estimate this proportion by selecting a random sample of shoppers, and using the proportion of shoppers in the sample who are female as an estimate of the proportion of all shoppers who are female. Which of the following is closest to the smallest sample size for which the owners can be at least 98% confident of getting an estimate that is within 0.05 of the true proportion?

(A) 105   (B) 136   (C) 385   (D) 422   (E) 543

Answer

10. There are more than 10 students in an AP Statistics class. Let the mean height of the students in the class be μ. The teacher will randomly select 10 students from the class. What further assumption, if any, is necessary in order to know that the expected value of the sample mean height is equal to μ?

(A) The heights of the students in the class are approximately normally distributed.
(B) After each selection, the student is replaced before making the next selection.
(C) The students are selected without replacement.
(D) The sample consists of less than 10% of the class.
(E) No further assumption is necessary.

Answer

11. For category VIIIa trucks undergoing emissions testing at a particular station, the carbon monoxide (CO) output in grams per mile has mean 2.395 and standard deviation 0.225. (Category VIIIa trucks are long-haul semi-tractor trailers.) The state administration is considering allowing road use only to those vehicles in this category whose CO emissions are 2.8 grams per mile or less.

Suppose that two category VIIIa trucks will be selected at random. Assuming that the carbon monoxide emissions are normally distributed for this category of truck, which of the following is closest to the probability that both of these trucks would, according to the new ruling, be allowed to continue using the roads?

(A) 0.883   (B) 0.929   (C) 0.942   (D) 0.964   (E) 0.991

Answer

12. It has been suggested that, if you lose your wallet, the wallet is more likely to be returned by the finder if it contains a photograph that will encourage the finder to react in a helpful way. In order to investigate this, an experiment will be performed. Using 240 identical wallets, 40 will contain a photograph of a baby, 40 will contain a photograph of a puppy, 40 will contain a photograph of a family, 40 will contain a photograph of an elderly couple, 40 will contain a card that indicates that the owner has recently donated to a charity, and 40 will contain no photograph or card. A return address will be included in every wallet. The wallets will then be dropped at random locations in a city. After three weeks, for each type of wallet, the number of wallets that have been returned, and the number that have not been returned, will be recorded.

The entire data set will be analyzed using a single hypothesis test. Which of the following would be the most suitable test to use?

(A) z test for a population mean
(B) z test for a population proportion
(C) Paired t test
(D) Chi-square test for goodness of fit
(E) Chi-square test for homogeneity

Answer

13. A chain of supermarkets has recently run a pilot program where virtually all checking out is done using self-checkout machines. In order to investigate customer satisfaction, a random sample of customers was selected, and each person in the sample was given questions to answer. A linear regression analysis was run using the variables "age" and "satisfaction," and part of the computer output is shown below.

```
Predictor     Coef        SE Coef       T          P
Constant      106.33      3.86          27.54      0.000
Age           -1.2430     0.0803        -15.48     0.000

S = 16.4298      R-Sq = 54.77%      R-Sq(adj) = 54.54%
```

Which of the following is/are true for this data set?

    I. The value of the correlation coefficient is 0.740.
   II. The slope of the least squares regression line is 16.4298.
  III. The y-intercept of the least squares regression line is 106.33.

(A) I only
(B) II only
(C) III only
(D) I and II only
(E) II and III only

Answer

14. Victor is taking a graduate class in college. There are 11 students in the class, and after the midterm exam the professor writes the scores on the blackboard in the form of a stemplot with the leaves written in order. Victor copies the stemplot, but is unfortunately unable to read two of the leaves. The stemplot is shown below, with the unknown leaves shown as X and Y. (Key: 6|7 represents an exam score of 67.)

$$
\begin{array}{c|cccc}
6 & 7 & X & & \\
7 & 1 & 3 & 6 & 8 \\
8 & 1 & 6 & 9 & \\
9 & 0 & Y & & \\
\end{array}
$$

What scores, represented by X and Y, would result in the greatest possible standard deviation of the exam scores for the class?

(A) 67 and 90
(B) 67 and 99
(C) 68 and 99
(D) 69 and 90
(E) 69 and 99

Answer

15. A bus company states that, on a particular route, "You can be 95% sure that your journey time will be between 90 and 120 minutes." This is

   (A)   a confidence interval for a mean
   (B)   a confidence interval for a proportion
   (C)   a confidence interval for a difference in means
   (D)   a confidence interval for a difference in proportions
   (E)   not a confidence interval

Answer

16. The giant toad, *bufo marinus*, is a species found in Southern Florida. A sample of 46 giant toads was selected, and the snout vent length (SVL) and the length of the right radioulna bone were measured in millimeters for each toad in the sample. The resulting scatterplot is shown below. (The least squares regression line for predicting the length of the radioulna bone has been added to the graph.)

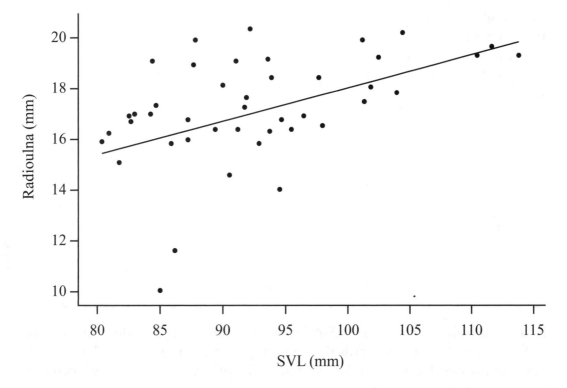

The value of the correlation coefficient for the two variables is $r = 0.481$.

Which of the following is true?

(A) There is a negative association between snout vent length and radioulna length.
(B) If radioulna was plotted on the horizontal axis and snout vent length was plotted on the vertical axis, the resulting value of r would be −0.481.
(C) If the residuals were to be calculated for all 46 points in the scatterplot then the mean residual would be negative.
(D) If the three points with the smallest radioulna values were to be removed from the scatterplot then the slope of the resulting least squares regression line would be positive, but smaller than for the original data set.
(E) If the three points with the smallest radioulna values were to be removed from the scatterplot then the slope of the resulting least squares regression line would be negative.

Answer

17. A random sample will be selected from the students at a large high school. Each student in the sample will be asked for his or her journey time to school, and the results will be used to construct a 95% confidence interval for the mean journey time for students at the school. If this process were to be repeated a large number of times, then approximately 95% of the confidence intervals would contain

(A) the population mean
(B) the sample mean
(C) the population standard deviation
(D) the sample standard deviation
(E) zero

Answer

18. Alex is taking a computer science course. He has written a program that, when he presses the "enter" key on his computer, records the decimal portion of the "seconds" part of the exact time when he presses that key. So, for example, if he presses the enter key when the exact time (by the computer's clock) is

2:31 and 24.326 seconds,

the computer records "0.326."

Alex cannot see the computer's clock. He will press the enter key 50 times at random, and he will then have the computer calculate the mean of the 50 results.

Consider now all the possible values of this mean. Of the distributions given below, which will provide the best approximation to the distribution of these values?

(A) A chi-square distribution
(B) A geometric distribution
(C) A normal distribution
(D) A t distribution
(E) A uniform distribution

Answer

19. In a particular country, a study using a sample of adult residents showed that those who had high daily intakes of water had healthier hearts, generally speaking, than those who had low water intake. An article on the Internet shortly after conclusion of the study was titled "Drink more water for a healthy heart!" However, it is known that, in that country, people who have a high water intake tend to exercise more than people with low water intake, and it is known that exercising promotes a healthy heart. It is also known that heart health is affected by genetic factors.

Which of the following are implied by the information given above?

     I. Exercise was a confounding variable in the study.
    II. Genetic factors were a confounding variable in the study.
    III. If the study could have been conducted using all adults in the country, there would be no possibility of confounding variables.

(A) I only
(B) III only
(C) I and II only
(D) II and III only
(E) I, II, and III

Answer

20. An experiment was conducted using adult volunteers to investigate the effects of diet on sleep. Treatment 1 consisted of a day of eating food provided by a nutritionist; the food was chosen to be high in protein and low in saturated fat. Treatment 2 consisted of a day of the participant eating his or her own choice of food. At the end of each day the participants were required to be in bed between 10 p.m. and 7 a.m., and the time taken for the participant to go to sleep was recorded. Using random assignment, some of the participants received Treatment 1 followed by Treatment 2, and the remaining participants received Treatment 2 followed by Treatment 1.

The analysis of the results will include a significance test to establish whether the results of the study provide convincing evidence of a smaller mean time to go to sleep after Treatment 1 than after Treatment 2 for adults like the ones in the study. Which of the following would NOT be an appropriate component of this analysis?

(A) Writing null and alternative hypotheses
(B) Calculating the difference (time to go to sleep after Treatment 1) – (time to go to sleep after Treatment 2) for each participant
(C) Checking that the time to go to sleep distributions for both treatments are roughly symmetrical and contain no outliers
(D) Calculating a t statistic
(E) Calculating a p-value

Answer

21. Justin has been asked to use a table of random digits to model the performance of a baseball batter. For this batter, the outcome of any "at bat" is exactly one of the following: "hit," "walk," or "out." For a randomly selected at bat, the probability that this batter gets a hit is 1/3 and the probability that he walks is 1/9. Which of the following would be a correct assignment of random digits for these outcomes?

(A) Take one digit at a time; 0–3 represent a hit, 4 represents a walk, and 5–9 represent being out.

(B) Take one digit at a time; 0–2 represent a hit, 3 represents a walk, 4–8 represent being out, and ignore 9.

(C) Take one digit at a time; 0–3 represent a hit, 4 represents a walk, 5–8 represent being out, and ignore 9.

(D) Take two digits at a time; 01–33 represent a hit, 34–44 represent a walk, and 00 and 45–99 represent being out.

(E) Take two digits at a time; 01–03 represent a hit, 04–12 represent a walk, 00 and 13–19 represent being out, and ignore all other pairs of digits.

Answer

22. Studies have shown that the hormone oxytocin is released during singing. (Oxytocin is known to reduce anxiety and stress, and oxytocin levels differ from person to person.) Let the standard deviation of the oxytocin levels for all adults involved in community singing be σ_X, and let the equivalent standard deviation for adults who do not sing be σ_Y. Suppose that an adult involved in community singing will be selected at random, and that person's oxytocin level, X, will be measured. Also, an adult who does not sing will be selected at random (independently of the choice of the singer), and that person's oxytocin level, Y, will also be measured. The standard deviation of all possible values of $X - Y$ is

(A) greater than σ_X and greater than σ_Y
(B) between σ_X and σ_Y
(C) less than σ_X and less than σ_Y
(D) equal to the larger of σ_X and σ_Y
(E) equal to the smaller of σ_X and σ_Y

Answer

Questions 23 and 24 refer to the following scenario.

As part of a biological study, a random sample of 15 adult meadow voles was selected, and the tails of the voles in the sample were measured. The results were used to conduct a t-test of the null hypothesis $H_0: \mu = 1.8$ against the alternative hypothesis $H_a: \mu > 1.8$, where μ is the mean tail length in inches for adult meadow voles in the area where the study was carried out. The conditions for conducting the hypothesis test were checked and found to be satisfied.

23. Which of the following is likely to have been the main reason for using a t distribution instead of a normal distribution for this hypothesis test?

   (A) t distribution probabilities are easier to calculate than normal distribution probabilities.
   (B) There could be large variability in tail length for the population of adult meadow voles.
   (C) The standardized test statistic involved an estimate of the population standard deviation.
   (D) The sampling distribution of the sample mean could not be assumed to be normal.
   (E) Tail-lengths for adult meadow voles in that area were unlikely to be normally distributed.

   Answer

24. The mean tail length for voles in the sample was 1.86 inches, and the p-value for the hypothesis test was 0.097. The value 0.097 is the probability

   (A) that the mean tail length for all adult meadow voles in the area is 1.8 given that the sample mean is 1.86
   (B) that the mean tail length for all adult meadow voles in the area is greater than 1.8 given that the sample mean is 1.86
   (C) of getting a sample mean equal to 1.86 given that the mean tail length for all adult meadow voles in the area is 1.8
   (D) of getting a sample mean greater than or equal to 1.86 given that the mean tail length for all adult meadow voles in the area is 1.8
   (E) of getting a sample mean equal to 1.86 given that the mean tail length for all adult meadow voles in the area is greater than 1.8

   Answer

25. Four students from School A and 8 students from School B attended a trivia competition. The mean and median scores for School A were both 26. The mean and median scores for School B were 30 and 32, respectively. Which of the following is true about the mean score and the median score for the combined group of 12 students?

(A) The mean is 28 and the median is 29.
(B) The mean is greater than 28 and the median is 29.
(C) The mean is 28, but the median cannot be determined from the information given.
(D) The mean is greater than 28, but the median cannot be determined from the information given.
(E) Neither the median nor the mean can be determined from the information given.

Answer

26. Using values from a random sample, a 95% confidence interval for a population mean μ was calculated to be (9.159, 10.195). Using the same sample values, a 99% confidence interval for μ was calculated to be (8.969, 10.385). Now, again using the same sample values, a hypothesis test will be conducted with hypotheses $H_0: \mu = 10$ *versus* $H_a: \mu \neq 10$. Which of the following could be the p-value for the test?

(A) 0.003   (B) 0.010   (C) 0.023   (D) 0.050   (E) 0.208

Answer

27. The figure below shows the graphs of the t distribution with 2 degrees of freedom (t_2), the t distribution with 4 degrees of freedom(t_4), and the normal distribution with mean 0 and standard deviation 1 ($N(0,1)$).

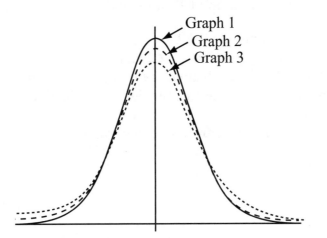

The three graphs are to be listed in order: Graph 1, Graph 2, Graph 3. Which of the following is correct?

(A) $t_2, t_4, N(0,1)$
(B) $t_4, t_2, N(0,1)$
(C) $N(0,1), t_2, t_4$
(D) $N(0,1), t_4, t_2$
(E) $t_2, N(0,1), t_4$

Answer

28. Stephanie did very well on a history test. In fact, the class was told the upper and lower quartile scores, and, using this information, Stephanie has worked out that her score was an outlier at the high end of the data set. However, the students who did least well are going to be allowed to take a retest. For these students, the new test score will count (whether it is higher or lower than the student's original score), except that no-one will be given a score that is higher than the original median. (Less than half of the class will take the retest.) Which of the following is true?

(A) If the lower quartile increases, then Stephanie's score will definitely still be an outlier.
(B) If the lower quartile increases, then Stephanie's score may or may not still be an outlier.
(C) If the lower quartile increases, then Stephanie's score will definitely not be an outlier.
(D) If the lower quartile decreases, then Stephanie's score will definitely still be an outlier.
(E) If the lower quartile decreases, then Stephanie's score will definitely not be an outlier.

Answer

29. When performing a chi-square test, a statistician will often check that all the expected counts are at least 5. The reason for this is that

(A) having large expected counts ensures a large number of degrees of freedom for the test
(B) large expected counts occur when the sample is large, and having a large sample ensures that the central limit theorem can be applied
(C) large expected counts occur when the sample is large, and having a large sample reduces bias in the sampling
(D) the distribution of the chi-square statistic can only be approximated well by a chi-square distribution if the expected counts are large enough
(E) in order to use a chi-square distribution, differences between the observed and expected counts need to be small, and the expected counts need to be large enough for this to be true

Answer

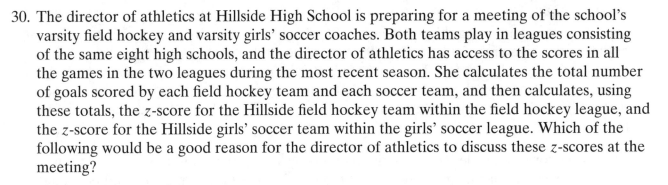

30. The director of athletics at Hillside High School is preparing for a meeting of the school's varsity field hockey and varsity girls' soccer coaches. Both teams play in leagues consisting of the same eight high schools, and the director of athletics has access to the scores in all the games in the two leagues during the most recent season. She calculates the total number of goals scored by each field hockey team and each soccer team, and then calculates, using these totals, the z-score for the Hillside field hockey team within the field hockey league, and the z-score for the Hillside girls' soccer team within the girls' soccer league. Which of the following would be a good reason for the director of athletics to discuss these z-scores at the meeting?

(A) She wants to show how close Hillside's field hockey scores were to being normally distributed, and to be able to give the same information for Hillside's soccer team.
(B) She wants to make it clear which of the two teams scored the most goals.
(C) She wants to discuss the season's results without mentioning which team did better.
(D) She wants to compare the two teams using statistics that are not affected by the performances of the other schools.
(E) She wants to make a fair comparison of the performance of the two teams.

Answer

31. Helen runs her business from home. On a randomly selected morning, the number of business calls she receives has the probability distribution shown below.

Number of Calls	0	1	2	3	4
Probability	0.24	0.32	0.21	0.15	0.08

Which of the following is a correct expression for the expected value of the number of calls on any given morning?

(A) $0(0.24) + 1(0.32) + 2(0.21) + 3(0.15) + 4(0.08)$

(B) $\dfrac{0 + 1 + 2 + 3 + 4}{5}$

(C) $\dfrac{0(0.24) + 1(0.32) + 2(0.21) + 3(0.15) + 4(0.08)}{5}$

(D) $\dfrac{0 + 1 + 2 + 34}{4}$

(E) $\dfrac{0(0.24) + 1(0.32) + 2(0.21) + 3(0.15) + 4(0.18)}{4}$

Answer

32. A company has a flexible approach to work hours, where office workers check in and check out using electronic cards, and, with certain restrictions, are free to do so when they want. The company's computers keep track of the workers' arrival and departure times, and calculate paychecks accordingly. An official from the company has been asked to report on the average time spent at work for the company's office workers during the previous month. Which of the following would be the most effective way of gathering this information?

(A) Select a simple random sample of office workers, and ask each person selected how many hours he or she worked during the previous month.

(B) Select a stratified random sample of office workers, stratifying by age and gender, and ask each person selected how many hours he or she worked during the previous month.

(C) Select a cluster sample of office workers, clustering by departure time, and ask each person selected how many hours he or she worked during the previous month.

(D) Between 4 p.m. and 5 p.m. on a Friday afternoon, ask office workers leaving the building how many hours they worked during the previous month.

(E) Use the computer records of the arrival and departure times of all office workers.

Answer

33. Orthopedic surgery treats problems that can develop in the bones, joints, and ligaments of the human body. Often, physical therapy is prescribed for patients who have undergone surgery of this sort; the physical therapy consists primarily of exercises done by the patient under the supervision of the physical therapist and at home.

A team of orthopedic physical therapists conducted a study of patient outcomes. Twenty patients were selected at random. After six weeks of physical therapy, each patient selected was asked to complete a questionnaire that assessed the degree to which the patient had completed the exercise program at home. This variable was called "completion." Additionally, without knowing the patients' responses to the questionnaire, the physical therapists assessed each patient's improvement. The initial results are shown in the first scatterplot below. Soon after this scatterplot was constructed, one patient showed a decline, and the results were updated, resulting in the second scatterplot. (The point for the patient whose results changed has been circled in each scatterplot.)

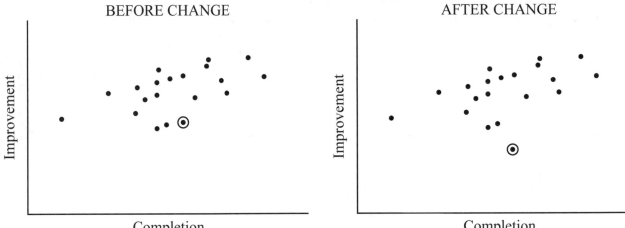

As a result of the change, the value of the coefficient of determination, r^2, has

(A) increased, because the slope of the least squares regression line relating improvement to completion is now greater

(B) increased, because the relationship between the two variables is now closer to being linear

(C) increased, because now a greater proportion of the variability in improvement can be explained by the least squares regression line relating improvement to completion

(D) decreased, because now a smaller proportion of the variability in completion and improvement can be explained by the least squares regression line relating improvement to completion

(E) decreased, because now a smaller proportion of the variability in improvement can be explained by the least squares regression line relating improvement to completion

Answer

34. At the election a year ago, a political party had the support of 38% of voters. A poll this week used a random sample of voters, and the proportion of voters showing support for the party was greater than 0.38, but not by a large enough margin to provide convincing evidence that the current support among the population of voters is greater than 38%. Which of the following could be true?

(A) Current support for the party is greater than 38%, and a Type I error occurred.
(B) Current support for the party is greater than 38%, and a Type II error occurred.
(C) Current support for the party is greater than 38%, and neither a Type I nor a Type II error occurred.
(D) Current support for the party is less than 38%, and a Type I error occurred.
(E) Current support for the party is less than 38%, and a Type II error occurred.

Answer

35. A study was conducted in a particular country over a period of 12 years using identical twins. The twins came from socioeconomic, ethnic, and racial backgrounds that were representative of the country as a whole. The study found that, among the twins who participated, if a child was more advanced in reading than his/her twin brother/sister at age 7, then, more likely than not, that person would be the more successful of the two on intelligence tests at age 16. The result was statistically significant. Which of the following is true?

(A) This was an experiment with a matched pairs design; it can be concluded that, for children in the country, being a good reader at age 7 causes high scores on intelligence tests at age 16.
(B) This was an experiment with a matched pairs design; it can be concluded that for the twins in the study, being a good reader at age 7 caused high scores on intelligence tests at age 16, but no conclusion can be made about causation for the country as a whole.
(C) This was an experiment with a matched pairs design; no conclusion about causation is possible.
(D) This was an observational study; the result of the study implies that for the twins in the study, being a good reader at age 7 caused high scores on intelligence tests at age 16.
(E) This was an observational study; no conclusion about causation can be made.

Answer

36. Upperdale Veterinary Center treats only cats and dogs. Thirty-two percent of the animals brought to the center are cats and the remainder are dogs. It is found that 52 percent of cats and 61 percent of dogs brought to the center show symptoms of flea allergy dermatitis. If an animal is selected at random from those that show symptoms of flea allergy dermatitis, what is the probability that the animal is a dog?

    (A) 0.585   (B) 0.610   (C) 0.714   (D) 0.782   (E) 0.819

Answer

37. A data set was compiled consisting of the birth weights of around 20,000 babies born after 32 weeks of gestation. The weights are summarized in the histogram below.

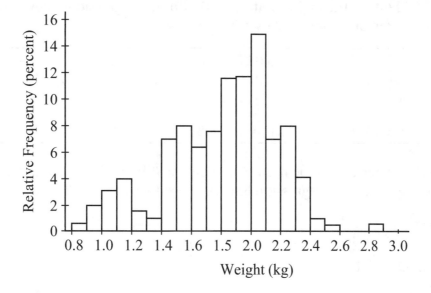

Which of the following is true about the distribution of weights?

(A) The distribution is positively skewed; the mean is less than the median.
(B) The distribution is positively skewed; there are more weights above the median than below the median.
(C) The distribution is negatively skewed; the mean is less than the median.
(D) The distribution is negatively skewed; the mean is greater than the median.
(E) The distribution is negatively skewed; there are more weights below the median than above the median.

Answer

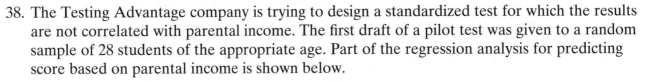

38. The Testing Advantage company is trying to design a standardized test for which the results are not correlated with parental income. The first draft of a pilot test was given to a random sample of 28 students of the appropriate age. Part of the regression analysis for predicting score based on parental income is shown below.

```
Term        Coef      SE Coef    T-Value    P-Value
Constant    40.19     8.90       4.51       0.000
Income      0.333     0.151      2.22       0.036

S = 9.07328      R-sq = 12.65%    R-sq(adj) = 15.88%
```

Which of the following should be used to compute a 99% confidence interval for the slope of the population least squares regression line for these two variables?

(A) $0.333 \pm 2.220 \times \dfrac{0.151}{\sqrt{28}}$

(B) $0.333 \pm 2.771 \times 0.151$

(C) $0.333 \pm 2.771 \times \dfrac{0.151}{\sqrt{28}}$

(D) $0.333 \pm 2.779 \times 0.151$

(E) $0.333 \pm 2.779 \times \dfrac{0.151}{\sqrt{28}}$

Answer

39. Of the following, which is most likely to be binomially distributed?

(A) The number of heads when five coins are flipped
(B) The number of flips of a coin until you get a head
(C) The score on the next roll of a number cube with faces numbered 1–6
(D) The proportion of the next eight rolls of a number cube for which the score is 6
(E) The length of the tail of the next dog you see

Answer

40. A company is testing a new medical procedure. The company has decided to run 10 identical experiments using different sets of experimental subjects. For each experiment, a hypothesis test will be conducted using a 5% significance level, with the null hypothesis that the procedure has no effect and the alternative hypothesis that the procedure has a positive effect. Suppose that in reality the procedure has no effect. What is the probability that at least one of the experiments will result in convincing evidence that the procedure has a positive effect?

(A) 0.032   (B) 0.315   (C) 0.401   (D) 0.500   (E) 0.642

Answer

SECTION II PART A

Questions 1–5
Spend about 65 minutes on this part of the exam.
Percent of Section II grade—75

Directions: Show all your work. Indicate clearly the methods you use, because you will be graded on the correctness of your method as well as on the accuracy and completeness of your results and explanations.

1. In an open water swim event there were 341 men and 216 women who finished. The time taken in minutes to complete the course was recorded for each participant. The times for the men and the women are summarized in the histograms below.

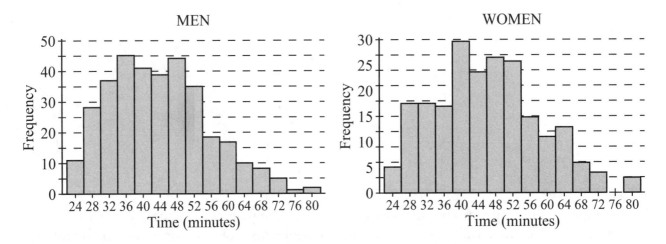

(a)   Which group – the men or the women – had the greater proportion of finishers completing the course in less than 34 minutes? Show the calculations that lead to your answer.

(b) Explain how you would use the histograms to estimate the median time for the male finishers and the median time for the female finishers. What are your estimates of these median times?

(c) Which group – the male finishers or the female finishers – produced the stronger performance in this event? Was there a large difference between the two groups? Justify your answer.

2. Members of the Onahu River All-Age Rowing Club regularly practice on indoor rowing machines, known as ergometers, or "ergs." The club keeps a record of the ages and the current best 2000-meter erg times for the members of the club. The most recent results are shown in the scatterplot below.

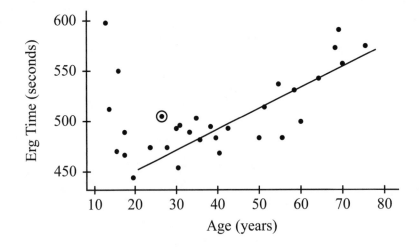

(a)   Describe how erg time is related to age for the members of this rowing club.

(b) Suppose that the least squares regression line for predicting erg times will be constructed for the rowers whose ages are between 20 and 80 years.

    i. Would this line provide a good description of the relationship between erg time and age for the rowers whose ages are less than 20 years? Explain your answer.

    ii. Would the residual for the circled point be positive or negative? Explain your answer.

3. An experiment was designed to investigate the effect of sleep on learning. The experiment was conducted using college students who volunteered to take part. The students were randomly assigned to a "sleep" group and a "no-sleep" group. Each student was given a list of items to memorize, and then was tested 11 hours later to find out how many of the items he or she could recall. (All the students were given the same list.) The students in the sleep group were given the list to memorize at 9:00 p.m. and tested at 8:00 a.m. the following morning, and the students in the no-sleep group were given the list to memorize at 9:00 a.m. and tested at 8:00 p.m. the same day.

The students in the sleep group had a significantly higher average on the test than those in the no-sleep group, and the conclusion of the study was that sleep aids learning.

(a) What were the explanatory and response variables in this study?

Explanatory variable:

Response variable:

(b) What/who were the experimental units?

(c) It has been suggested that the time of day at which the students were tested was a confounding variable in this study. Argue convincingly that the time of day at which the students were tested was a confounding variable. Why does the presence of this confounding variable make it incorrect to conclude that sleep aids learning?

4. The speeds of the cars on a particular highway have mean 67 mph and standard deviation 4.8 mph.

(a)   Suppose that the police decide to pull over the fastest 1% of cars on this highway. Assuming that the speeds of the cars on the highway are normally distributed, what would be the minimum speed required in order to be pulled over?

Five percent of the cars on the highway have speeds greater than 75 mph. A random sample of 300 cars will be selected.

(b)   Let $\hat{p}$ be the proportion of cars in the sample that have speeds greater than 75 mph. Describe the sampling distribution of $\hat{p}$ in terms of shape, center, and spread. Justify your answer.

(c) Using your answer to part (b), calculate the approximate probability that more than 6% of the cars in the sample will have speeds greater than 75 mph.

5. A recent report by a national newspaper stated that, for the country as a whole, the average number of hours worked per week by full-time employees is 46.7 hours. A reporter for the Greenville Gazette, the local newspaper for the town of Greenville, is preparing a follow-up report. The reporter has selected a random sample of 15 full-time employees in Greenville. The numbers of hours of work per week for these 15 people are shown below.

36   61   53   39   45   48   47   49   33   37   52   33   43   56   38

A hypothesis test will be performed to determine whether these data provide convincing evidence that the mean number of hours worked per week for full-time employees in Greenville is different from the mean number of hours for the country as a whole.

(a)   The null and alternative hypotheses $H_0: \mu = 46.7$ *versus* $H_a: \mu \neq 46.7$ will be used for this hypothesis test. What does μ represent in this context?

(b)   Perform the remaining steps of the hypothesis test.

SECTION II PART B

Question 6
Spend about 25 minutes on this part of the exam.
Percent of Section II grade—25

Directions: Show all your work. Indicate clearly the methods you use, because you will be graded on the correctness of your method as well as on the accuracy and completeness of your results and explanations.

6. A communications company is conducting research concerning cellphone use. A questionnaire will be created in which, along with answering other questions, participants will state their age and will answer the following question:

"A friend is going to drive you to a social event. You need to contact the friend to arrange a time and a place to meet. Would you call your friend or would you send a text?"

Linda, an employee of the company, is asked to conduct an initial survey using 120 participants. Assume that the participants will be selected at random. The results of the survey will be written in a table such as the one shown below. (Each star will be replaced by the number of people in that category.)

TABLE 1

		Response	
		Would Call	Would Text
Age	24 or under	★	★
	25 or over	★	★

A chi-square test for independence will then be performed.

(a) Write the null and alternative hypotheses for this significance test.

It is suggested to Linda that the true proportions of the population of cellphone users for the four categories are as shown in the table below.

TABLE 2

		Response	
		Would Call	Would Text
Age	24 or under	0.09	0.27
	25 or over	0.32	.032

(b)   Assume that the information in Table 2 is correct and that a cellphone user will be selected at random. Are the events "24 or under" and "would call" independent? Explain your answer.

Linda will estimate the probability that her survey will result in the null hypothesis being rejected, given that the information in Table 2 is correct.

(c)   Explain the relevance of this probability.

Using a computer, Linda simulates the responses of a sample of 120 people, assuming that the information in Table 2 is correct. She gets the results shown in the table below.

TABLE 3

		Response	
		Would Call	Would Text
Age	24 or under	12	32
	25 or over	36	40

(d) A chi-square test for independence is conducted using the results in Table 3.
  i. Calculate the p-value for this hypothesis test.

  ii. A 5% significance level will be used. Will the null hypothesis be rejected? Explain briefly.

Linda now uses the computer to simulate 20 samples of 120 people each, assuming that the information in Table 2 is correct. She has the computer determine, for each sample, whether the null hypothesis would be rejected or not rejected. Her results are shown below.

Sample	Result of Hypothesis Test
1	Reject H_0
2	Do not reject H_0
3	Reject H_0
4	Reject H_0
5	Do not reject H_0
6	Do not reject H_0
7	Reject H_0
8	Reject H_0
9	Reject H_0
10	Reject H_0
11	Do not reject H_0
12	Reject H_0
13	Do not reject H_0
14	Do not reject H_0
15	Reject H_0
16	Do not reject H_0
17	Do not reject H_0
18	Reject H_0
19	Reject H_0
20	Reject H_0

(e) According to the results of these 20 simulated samples, what should be Linda's estimate of the probability that H_0 will be rejected? In light of this probability, should Linda redesign the study? Explain your answer.

SAMPLE EXAMINATION THREE
SECTION I

Time—1 hour and 30 minutes
Number of questions—40
Percent of total grade—50

Directions: Solve each of the following problems, using the available space for scratch work. Decide which is the best of the choices given and fill in the corresponding oval on the answer sheet. No credit will be given for anything written in the test book. Do not spend too much time on any one problem.

1. A used car salesman deals in sedans and SUVs, and keeps note of the horsepower of each vehicle. The values for his current inventory are represented by the boxplots below.

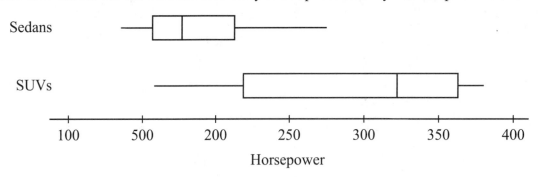

Which of the following is true?

(A) The distribution for the sedans is positively skewed and the distribution for the SUVs is negatively skewed. The range is greater for the sedans than for the SUVs.
(B) The distribution for the sedans is negatively skewed and the distribution for the SUVs is positively skewed. The range is greater for the sedans than for the SUVs.
(C) The distribution for the sedans is positively skewed and the distribution for the SUVs is negatively skewed. The range is less for the sedans than for the SUVs.
(D) The distribution for the sedans is negatively skewed and the distribution for the SUVs is positively skewed. The range is less for the sedans than for the SUVs.
(E) Both distributions are roughly symmetrical. The range is greater for the sedans than for the SUVs.

Answer

2. In order to study the effects of organic feed on the health of animals, some cows from a herd are randomly selected to be given organic feed, while the remaining cows are given a non-organic equivalent. At the end of the study the health levels of all the cows are measured. Which of the following is true?

(A) This is an observational study in which the level of health is the explanatory variable and the type of feed is the response variable.
(B) This is an observational study in which the type of feed is the explanatory variable and the level of health is the response variable.
(C) This is an observational study that could establish whether organic feed causes good health.
(D) This is an experiment in which the level of health is the explanatory variable and the type of feed is the response variable.
(E) This is an experiment in which the type of feed is the explanatory variable and the level of health is the response variable.

Answer

3. Of the male students at a high school, 35% play football, 44% play basketball, and 12% play both of these sports. If a male student is chosen at random, what is the probability that he plays exactly one of the sports?

(A) 0.482   (B) 0.55   (C) 0.636   (D) 0.67   (E) 0.79

Answer

4. A confidence interval will be used to estimate a population proportion. If a random sample of size 50 and a random sample of size 200 are selected, and 90% and 95% confidence intervals for the population proportion are calculated for each sample, which of the four confidence intervals is likely to be the narrowest?

(A) The 90% confidence interval for the smaller sample
(B) The 95% confidence interval for the smaller sample
(C) The 90% confidence interval for the larger sample
(D) The 95% confidence interval for the larger sample
(E) The two 95% confidence intervals, they being likely to have roughly equal widths

Answer

5. For a set of 15 decathletes, the correlation between their times for the 100 meter sprint and their distances in the long jump was -0.675. The standard deviation of their 100 meter times was 0.383 seconds and the standard deviation of their long jump distances was 0.469 meters. Denoting 100 meter time by x and long jump distance by y, what is the slope of the least squares regression line of y on x?

(A) -1.012 (B) -0.827 (C) -0.675 (D) -0.551 (E) -0.450

Answer

6. A polling organization is given the job of assessing whether the proportions of homemakers using various types of cooking oil are changing during an advertising campaign. A random sample of homemakers is selected before the campaign starts, and each homemaker in the sample is asked whether he/she primarily uses canola oil, olive oil, sunflower oil, or some other sort of oil for cooking. After the first stage of the campaign, a new random sample of homemakers is selected, and the people selected are asked the same question as those in the first sample. After the final stage of the campaign, a third random sample of homemakers is selected, and the people selected are asked the same question. Which of the following would be most suitable for analysis of the results of this study?

(A) One-sample z-test for a proportion
(B) Two-sample t-test for means
(C) Paired t-test
(D) Chi-square test for goodness of fit
(E) Chi-square test for homogeneity

Answer

7. In an election, the Democratic candidate received 799,072 votes, the Republican candidate received 783,426 votes, and the other two candidates received a combined total of 157,302 votes. These results could be appropriately represented using

(A) a stemplot
(B) a histogram
(C) a pie chart
(D) a boxplot
(E) a scatterplot

Answer

8. It is known that 68% of the adult residents of a large town are male, and that 90% of the adult male residents are employed and 76% of the adult female residents are employed. A random sample of 800 adult residents of the town is selected. Which of the following is closest to the expected number of people in the sample who are employed?

(A) 644   (B) 654   (C) 664   (D) 674   (E) 684

Answer

9. A particular ski slope is used by a large number of people. A researcher wishes to establish whether there is a difference between the mean times taken to complete the descent for men and women. In order to answer this question, independent random samples of men and women using the slope are selected and the times are recorded for the people selected. Let μ_M represent the mean time for all men and let μ_W represent the mean time for all women. If the results of the study are to be analyzed using a hypothesis test, what hypotheses should be used?

(A) $H_0: \mu_M = \mu_W$, $H_a: \mu_M \neq \mu_W$

(B) $H_0: \mu_M = \mu_W$, $H_a: \mu_M > \mu_W$

(C) $H_0: \mu_D = 0$, $H_a: \mu_D \neq 0$

(D) $H_0: \mu_D = 0$, $H_a: \mu_D > 0$

(E) $H_0: \mu_M > \mu_W$, $H_a: \mu_M < \mu_W$

Answer

10. Garden Delicious pea pods have lengths that are approximately normally distributed with standard deviation 0.8 inches. The largest 1 percent of pods are eligible for prizes. How many inches above the mean pod length is the smallest pod that is eligible for a prize?

(A) 1.64   (B) 1.86   (C) 1.94   (D) 2.02   (E) 2.33

Answer

11. Larry is enrolled in four academic classes. The grades for all the students in Larry's four classes are represented by the boxplots shown below. (The boxplot for the students in Larry's English class shows one outlier, represented by a dot.)

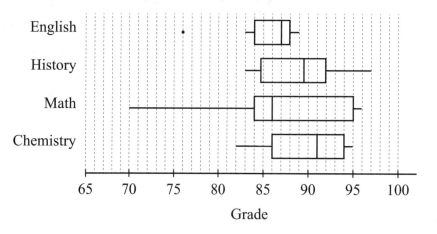

Larry's grades are 84 in English, 88 in History, 86 in Math, and 92 in Chemistry. His advisor decides to list the four classes according to how well Larry performed relative to his fellow students, with the class in which Larry performed best (relative to his fellow students) showing first in the list. Which of the following is the correct list?

(A) Chemistry, English, Math, History
(B) Math, Chemistry, English, History
(C) Chemistry, Math, English, History
(D) Math, Chemistry, History, English
(E) Chemistry, Math, History, English

Answer

12. A hypothesis test is performed using the results of a random sample from a large population. The test is based on the null hypothesis, H_0, that a population parameter takes a particular value, and the alternative hypothesis, H_a, that the parameter does not take that value. Which of the following is true?

(A) The results could provide convincing evidence that the null hypothesis is true.
(B) The results could provide convincing evidence that the alternative hypothesis is true.
(C) The results could prove that the alternative hypothesis is false.
(D) The null hypothesis can only be rejected if it is false.
(E) Failure to reject the null hypothesis means that the null hypothesis is true.

Answer

13. Suppose that it is known that 13% of people are left-handed. If ten people are chosen at random, what is the probability that exactly two of them are left-handed?

(A) $\dfrac{1}{10}\dbinom{10}{2}$

(B) $(0.13)^2 (0.87)^8$

(C) $(0.87)^2 (0.13)^8$

(D) $\dbinom{10}{2}(0.13)^2 (0.87)^8$

(E) $\dbinom{10}{2}(0.87)^2 (0.13)^8$

Answer

14. A large Internet-based company serving the USA wishes to send a survey to a sample of its customers. Which of the following will result in a stratified random sample?

    (A)   Sending the survey to the next 4000 customers who place orders

    (B)   Numbering a complete list of customers sequentially and using a computer to randomly select 4000 customers from the list

    (C)   Numbering a complete list of customers sequentially and sending the survey to the customers numbered 258, 1258, 2258, 3258, and so on

    (D)   Dividing the country into a large number of regions, randomly selecting 30 of those regions, and sending the survey to all the customers in those 30 regions

    (E)   Dividing the customers into four separate groups according to the type of goods primarily ordered, and randomly selecting 1000 customers from each group

Answer

15. For a classroom activity, a teacher uses a bag containing 300 blue chips and 200 red chips. The teacher demonstrates the process of picking ten chips at random from the bag (replacing the chips and mixing between picks) and calculating the proportion of the ten chips that are blue. The students then repeat this process a large number of times, keeping note of the proportion of the ten chips that are blue on each occasion. The standard deviation of all the proportions calculated is likely to be closest to which of the following?

    (A) $\sqrt{\dfrac{(0.6)(0.4)}{10}}$

    (B) $\sqrt{10(0.6)(0.4)}$

    (C) $\sqrt{\dfrac{(0.6)(0.4)}{500}}$

    (D) $\sqrt{500(0.6)(0.4)}$

    (E) $\dfrac{(0.6)(0.4)}{\sqrt{500}}$

Answer

16. A random sample of size 8 has been selected from a large population, and the sample mean, $\bar{x}$, and the sample standard deviation, s, have been calculated. The population standard deviation is unknown. A confidence interval for the population mean is to be constructed. What is the correct formula to use, and what assumption has to be made about the population?

(A) $\bar{x} \pm z^* \cdot \dfrac{\sigma}{\sqrt{8}}$; no assumption about the about the population is necessary

(B) $\bar{x} \pm z^* \cdot \dfrac{s}{\sqrt{8}}$; we have to assume that the population is normally distributed

(C) $\bar{x} \pm t^* \cdot \dfrac{\sigma}{\sqrt{8}}$; no assumption about the about the population is necessary

(D) $\bar{x} \pm t^* \cdot \dfrac{s}{\sqrt{8}}$; no assumption about the about the population is necessary

(E) $\bar{x} \pm t^* \cdot \dfrac{s}{\sqrt{8}}$; we have to assume that the population is normally distributed

Answer

17. Frequently, experiments are designed to take account of the fact that many people show improvement resulting purely from the psychological effect of taking tablets, even if the tablets contain no active ingredient.

In an experiment, the subjects are randomly assigned to two groups. The people in one of the groups (the "treatment group") are given tablets containing a new drug. The people in the other group (the "placebo group") are given tablets that look and taste exactly the same as the other tablets, but contain no active ingredient. In order that the experiment should test the effectiveness of the drug, the experimental design depends on the fact that

(A) subjects in both groups could experience the potentially positive psychological effect of taking tablets
(B) only subjects in the placebo group could experience the potentially positive psychological effect of taking tablets
(C) only subjects in the treatment group could experience the potentially positive psychological effect of taking tablets
(D) no subject in the experiment will experience the potentially positive psychological effect of taking tablets
(E) nobody could ever experience a positive psychological effect as a result of taking tablets

Answer

Questions 18 and 19 refer to the following scenario and numerical information.

Eighty runners took part in a cross country race. Their times are summarized in the table below.

Time (minutes)	16	18	20	22	24	26	28	30	32
Cumulative Relative Frequency	0.000	0.0750	0.2625	0.5125	0.7125	0.8250	0.9375	0.9750	1.000

(The cumulative relative frequencies refer to the proportions of runners whose times were less than or equal to the times given.)

18. How many runners had times that were more than 20 minutes and at most 22 minutes?

(A) 10   (B) 20   (C) 30   (D) 40   (E) 50

Answer

19. Which of the following could be the interquartile range of the times?

(A) 3 minutes, 50 seconds
(B) 4 minutes, 40 seconds
(C) 8 minutes, 20 seconds
(D) 10 minutes, 30 seconds
(E) 12 minutes, 10 seconds

Answer

20. A random sample of 50 Brand A light bulbs and an independent random sample of 45 Brand B light bulbs were selected, and the lives (in hours) of the bulbs in the samples were measured. The partial computer output below shows the results of a test of H_0: $\mu_A = \mu_B$ versus H_a: $\mu_A \neq \mu_B$.

```
Two-sample T for Brand A vs Brand B

             N      Mean       StDev       SE Mean
Brand A     50      907.6      60.2        8.5
Brand B     45      890.8      46.0        6.9

Difference = mu (Brand A) - mu (Brand B)

T-Test of difference = 0 (vs not =):
T-Value = 1.54    P-Value = 0.127    DF = 90
```

Which of the following is NOT true?

(A) H_0 is not rejected at the 0.05 significance level.
(B) The value 1.54 is less than the positive critical value of a t distribution with 90 degrees of freedom for a single-tail probability of 0.025.
(C) A 95% two-sample t confidence interval based on these results would contain zero.
(D) If the population means were equal, the probability of getting a t statistic whose absolute value is at least 1.54 would be 0.127.
(E) Given a difference in sample means of 16.8, the probability that the population means are equal is 0.127.

Answer

21. Three statistics, Statistic 1, Statistic 2, and Statistic 3, are to be compared as estimators of a particular population parameter. To estimate the behavior of the statistics, 600 random samples are selected from the population, and the value of each statistic is calculated for each sample. The true value of the population parameter is 5. The distributions of the values of the three statistics are shown in the graphs below.

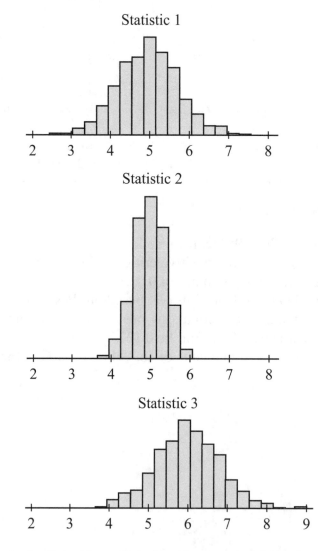

The three statistics are to be listed in order of preference, with the best statistic first in the list. Which of the following is correct?

(A) 1, 2, 3   (B) 2, 1, 3   (C) 1, 3, 2   (D) 3, 1, 2   (E) 2, 3, 1

Answer

22. A simple random sample of size 50 is selected from a population, and a measurement is taken for each individual in the sample. These results will be used to test the null hypothesis $H_0: \mu = 8$ *versus* the alternative hypothesis $H_a: \mu > 8$. A significance level of $\alpha = 0.05$ will be used for the test. Assuming that the true value of the population mean, μ, is greater than 8, which of the following would produce a test that has greater power than the one given above?

    I. Changing the significance level to $\alpha = 0.1$

    II. Changing the alternative hypothesis to $H_a: \mu \neq 8$

    III. Increasing the sample size to 100

(A) I only   (B) II only   (C) III only   (D) I and III   (E) II and III

Answer

23. A survey is to be designed in order to estimate some quantities associated with a population. Which of the following is NOT true?

(A) A census will always be more representative of the population than a sample.

(B) How well a sample will represent the population is influenced by the quality of the sampling method used.

(C) How well a random sample will represent the population is partly a matter of chance.

(D) A simple random sample will always represent the population better than a systematic sample.

(E) A convenience sample is unlikely to be representative of the population.

Answer

24. In a particular state, it is known that 40% of daily trips are for shopping or running errands, 30% are for social or recreational purposes, 18% are for commuting to work, and 12% are for other purposes. A survey in one town within the state included 500 daily trips, of which 192 were for shopping or running errands, 133 were for social or recreational purposes, 118 were for commuting to work, and 57 were for other purposes. A hypothesis test is conducted in order to find out whether the pattern of daily trips for the town differs from the pattern for the state as a whole. (The test is based on the assumption that the 500 daily trips in the survey form a random sample of the daily trips for the town.) What is the value of the test statistic?

(A) 1.59 (B) 5.03 (C) 8.23 (D) 9.31 (E) 11.11

Answer

25. It is known that one-fifth of the vehicles that pass a particular intersection are commercial vehicles, and that the vehicles pass this intersection independently. A student is planning to stand at the intersection and count the vehicles that pass up to and including the first commercial vehicle. Which of the following best describes the distribution of the number of vehicles the student will count?

(A) Binomial
(B) Chi-square
(C) Geometric
(D) Normal
(E) t

Answer

26. The management of a factory wishes to compare a new machine for producing saucers with the machine the factory currently uses for that purpose. Random samples of 80 saucers from the new machine and 100 saucers from the current machine are selected, and it is found that 17 of the saucers from the new machine and 28 of the saucers from the current machine have faults. The new machine will be incorporated if, and only if, these results provide convincing evidence at the 0.05 significance level that the proportion of faulty saucers is less for the new machine than for the current machine. Will the new machine be incorporated?

(A) Yes, because $P\left(z < \dfrac{0.2125 - 0.28}{\sqrt{\dfrac{(0.2125)(0.7875)}{80} + \dfrac{(0.28)(0.72)}{100}}}\right)$ is greater than 0.05.

(B) No, because $P\left(z < \dfrac{0.2125 - 0.28}{\sqrt{\dfrac{(0.2125)(0.7875)}{80} + \dfrac{(0.28)(0.72)}{100}}}\right)$ is greater than 0.05.

(C) Yes, because $P\left(z < \dfrac{0.2125 - 0.28}{\sqrt{(0.25)(0.75)\left(\dfrac{1}{80} + \dfrac{1}{100}\right)}}\right)$ is greater than 0.05.

(D) No, because $P\left(z < \dfrac{0.2125 - 0.28}{\sqrt{(0.25)(0.75)\left(\dfrac{1}{80} + \dfrac{1}{100}\right)}}\right)$ is greater than 0.05.

(E) Yes, because $P\left(z < \dfrac{0.2125 - 0.28}{\sqrt{(0.25)(0.75)\left(\dfrac{1}{80} + \dfrac{1}{100}\right)}}\right)$ is less than 0.05.

Answer

Questions 27 and 28 refer to the following scenario and numerical information.

The department of transportation for a particular state kept records of the number of new cars sold (x) and the number of used cars sold (y) for each month last year. Some computer output from a regression analysis of these data is shown below.

```
Dependent variable: Number of used cars sold

Predictor    Coef       StDev      T         P
Constant     32971      9656       3.41      0.007
New_cars     0.8566     0.4593     1.86      0.092

S = 5418.57      R-Sq = 25.8%      R-Sq(adj) = 18.4%
```

27. During the month of July, 22,836 new cars and 57,693 used cars were sold. What is the residual for this data point?

(A) 5161   (B) −5161   (C) 5323   (D) −5323   (E) −5774

Answer

28. Treating the twelve months last year as a random sample of all months, and assuming that the other conditions for inference are met, at what level of significance do last year's results provide evidence of a non-zero slope in the population regression line of y on x?

(A) At the 0.01 level
(B) At the 0.05 level, but not at the 0.01 level
(C) At the 0.1 level, but not at the 0.05 level
(D) At the 0.05 level, but not at the 0.1 level
(E) Not at any reasonable significance level

Answer

29. Which of the following could be conducted in a double-blind manner?

(A) An experiment to investigate whether listening to music while typing increases the number of errors made
(B) An experiment to investigate whether regular exercise reduces blood pressure
(C) An experiment to investigate whether taking vitamin C speeds recovery from a cold
(D) An experiment to investigate whether drinking sufficient quantities of water increases the effectiveness of food supplements
(E) An experiment to investigate whether use of keyboard shortcuts reduces the time taken to perform a particular computer task

Answer

30. A transportation authority conducts a survey of users of a commuter railroad. A random sample of passengers is selected, and each passenger in the sample is given a questionnaire. There are two questions on the questionnaire. The first question asks whether the passenger paid for the journey at the ticket office, using a machine located on the platform, or online. The second question asks how happy the passenger is with the transportation service (very happy, happy, neutral, or unhappy). A hypothesis test will be conducted to determine whether there is an association between the method of payment and happiness with the service. The test will use a chi-square distribution with k degrees of freedom. What is the value of k?

(A) 2   (B) 3   (C) 6   (D) 9   (E) 12

Answer

31. After a successful year, a company decides to increase the salaries of all of its employees by 5 percent. Which of the following will NOT be increased by 5 percent?

(A) The mean salary
(B) The standard deviation of the salaries
(C) The variance of the salaries
(D) The median salary
(E) The interquartile range of the salaries

Answer

32. An experiment is to be designed to compare the side-effects associated with a new drug with those associated with a current drug designed for the same purpose. It is accepted that the older a person is, the more likely it is that the person will be negatively affected by these drugs. The designers of the experiment therefore decide to block by age. This blocking will ensure that

(A) all the older people will receive one of the drugs, with the younger people receiving the other drug
(B) in terms of age, the people who receive the new drug are different from the people who receive the current drug
(C) in terms of age, the people who receive the new drug are similar to the people who receive the current drug
(D) the people who take the current drug will be similar to each other with respect to age, and the people who take the new drug will be similar to each other with respect to age
(E) the assignment of the subjects to the two drugs is completely random

Answer

33. In the context of linear regression, an influential point is a data point whose removal would have a large effect on the least squares regression line of y on x. For reasonably large data sets, which of the following are true?

    I. Any point with a large residual is an influential point.

    II. Any point that is an outlier in the x-direction is an influential point.

    III. Removal of an influential point could increase the absolute value of the correlation coefficient.

(A) II only
(B) III only
(C) I and II only
(D) II and III only
(E) I, II, and III

Answer

34. It is estimated that, for the people in a large community, the standard deviation of the daily calorie intake is 245. Assuming that this standard deviation is correct, how large a random sample of people from the community would be necessary in order to estimate the mean daily calorie intake to within 30 calories with 95% confidence?

(A) 17   (B) 131   (C) 257   (D) 308   (E) 3922

Answer

35. Two blue cubes and three green cubes, each with faces labeled 1–6, will be rolled. Letting X be the total score for the two blue cubes and Y be the total score for the three green cubes, it can be shown that the standard deviations of the random variables X and Y are 2.42 and 2.96, respectively. Which of the following is the standard deviation of $X - Y$?

(A) -2.91 (B) -0.54 (C) 3.82   (D) 4.68   (E) 14.62

Answer

36. A statistics question requires a significance test with null hypothesis H_0: $p = 0.3$, where p is a population proportion. Two students, Juan and Tamara, both do the question, and they both calculate the correct positive value of the z-statistic. However, Juan performs a one-tailed test (using the alternative hypothesis H_a: $p > 0.3$), and Tamara performs a two-tailed test (using the alternative hypothesis H_a: $p \neq 0.3$). Given that both students are correct in their work, which of the following is NOT possible?

(A) Both students reject the null hypothesis at the 0.05 significance level.
(B) Both students fail to reject the null hypothesis at the 0.05 significance level.
(C) Juan rejects the null hypothesis at the 0.05 significance level and Tamara fails to reject the null hypothesis at the 0.05 significance level.
(D) Juan fails to reject the null hypothesis at the 0.05 significance level and Tamara rejects the null hypothesis at the 0.05 significance level.
(E) Juan fails to reject the null hypothesis at the 0.01 significance level and Tamara rejects the null hypothesis at the 0.05 significance level.

Answer

37. A random sample will be selected from a population of rabbits. The weights of the rabbits in the sample will be measured, and the sample mean weight will be calculated. Assuming that the sample size is greater than 1, the standard deviation of the sampling distribution of the sample mean is

(A) less than the population standard deviation, because the weight of any rabbit in the sample is likely to be closer to the population mean than the weight of a rabbit chosen at random from the population
(B) less than the population standard deviation, because, when calculating the sample mean, weights in the sample far from the population mean are averaged out with the other weights in the sample
(C) equal to the population standard deviation
(D) more than the population standard deviation, because there is a greater possibility of getting a weight that is far from the population mean in the sample than when picking one rabbit at random
(E) more than the population standard deviation, because using a large sample introduces a greater possibility of the sample mean being far from the population mean

Answer

38. A statistics teacher calculates the correlation between the heights (in inches) and the weights (in pounds) of the students in her class. Which of the following would change the value of the correlation coefficient?

(A) Adding 5 inches to each height
(B) Subtracting 10 pounds from each weight
(C) Adding 5 inches to each height and subtracting 10 pounds from each weight
(D) Subtracting each height from 100
(E) Converting the heights to centimeters

Answer

39. An article describes a *t*-test of $H_0 : \mu = 20$ *versus* $H_a : \mu > 20$, and the value of the test statistic is given to be 1.58. The sample size is not given in the article, but is known to be between 5 and 30 inclusive. Assuming that all the conditions for inference are met, the *p*-value for the test would be

(A) less than 0.01
(B) between 0.01 and 0.05
(C) between 0.05 and 0.1
(D) between 0.1 and 0.2
(E) greater than 0.2

Answer

40. The ethnic breakdown of a particular county is known to be as follows: Caucasian: 38%, Hispanic: 34%, African American: 16%, and Asian: 12%. If two people are chosen at random from this county, what is the approximate probability that they are of the same ethnicity? (The population of the county can be assumed to be large.)

(A) 0.28   (B) 0.30   (C) 0.32   (D) 0.34   (E) 0.36

Answer

NO TESTING MATERIAL ON THIS PAGE

SECTION II PART A

Questions 1–5
Spend about 65 minutes on this part of the exam.
Percent of Section II grade—75

Directions: Show all your work. Indicate clearly the methods you use, because you will be graded on the correctness of your method as well as on the accuracy and completeness of your results and explanations.

1. The graphical display below shows the proportions of male and female students in the undergraduate, master's, and doctoral programs at a particular university. These are the only three programs available at this university.

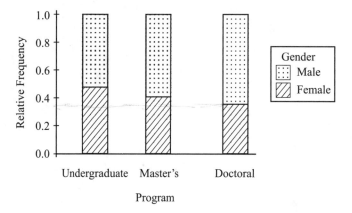

(a) What does the display reveal about the way gender balance varies among the three programs?

(b)   Does the information in the display imply that the number of males in the doctoral program is greater than the number of males in the masters program? Explain.

(c)   When selecting a student at random from the university, are the events "is enrolled in the doctoral program" and "is female" mutually exclusive? Justify your answer.

(d)   When selecting a student at random from the university, are the events "is enrolled in the doctoral program" and "is female" independent? Justify your answer.

2. A study concluded that AP students who attend extra study sessions do better, on average, on their AP exams than students who do not attend extra study sessions.

   (a) Explain why we cannot conclude from the result of the study that attending extra study sessions *causes* increased AP scores. Include an example of a plausible confounding variable.

   An experiment is designed where 200 AP students will be randomly assigned to two groups (Group A and Group B), each of size 100. The students in Group A will be required to attend extra study sessions, while those in Group B will not be given that opportunity.

   (b) Explain how the 200 students might be randomly assigned to the two treatment groups.

(c) Suppose that the students in Group A receive significantly higher AP results, on average, than the students in Group B. Explain why we now *do* have evidence that attending extra study sessions increases AP scores.

3. For every household in a particular county, the water use (in thousands of gallons) over the course of a year was recorded. The mean water use for the households in the county was found to be 162 and the standard deviation was 140.

    (a)   Based on the information given above, could the distribution of household water use for that county be approximately normal? Explain your answer.

    (b)   A random sample of 50 households will be selected, and the mean water use will be calculated for the households in the sample. Is the sampling distribution of the sample mean for random samples of size 50 approximately normal? Explain.

(c)   Suppose that the annual indoor water use (in thousands of gallons) for the same county is approximately normally distributed with mean 57 and standard deviation 12. If a random sample of 50 households is selected, what is the probability that their mean indoor water use (in thousands of gallons) will be greater than 59?

4. Random samples of 48 girls and 45 boys were selected from a large school district. It was found that 37 of the girls and 20 of the boys were not consuming the recommended amount of vitamin A.

(a) Use a 95% confidence interval to estimate the difference between the proportions of girls and boys in the school district who do not consume the recommended amount of vitamin A.

(b) Based only on this confidence interval, do you think that there is a difference between the proportions of girls and boys in the district who are not consuming the recommended amount of vitamin A? Justify your answer.

5. Exposure of workers to asbestos at construction sites and shipyards is considered dangerous. The workers at a construction site are concerned that asbestos might be present in the air, and so an inspector has been called. The inspector will select a random sample of locations at the site and will measure the asbestos level at those locations. If the data collected by the inspector provide convincing evidence that mean level of asbestos at the site is below the permissible exposure limit of 0.1 fibers per cubic centimeter (f/cc) then work at the site will be allowed to continue. Otherwise, work will stop until precautions have been put into place.

(a) The results of the inspection will be analyzed by means of a hypothesis test. State the null and alternative hypotheses that would be used for the test, and define the parameter of interest.

(b) In the context of this situation, describe Type I and Type II errors and describe the consequences for the workers of each type of error.

SECTION II PART B

Question 6
Spend about 25 minutes on this part of the exam.
Percent of Section II grade—25

Directions: Show all your work. Indicate clearly the methods you use, because you will be graded on the correctness of your method as well as on the accuracy and completeness of your results and explanations.

6. A meteorological organization records the daily temperatures at noon (local time) at various locations across the world. A time plot for the temperatures at Location A last year is shown below. (The days of the year are numbered 1 through 365, with "1" representing January 1st, and "365" representing December 31st. The days are shown on the horizontal axis, and, for each day, a single point is plotted showing the temperature for that day.) Additionally, a histogram summarizing the Location A temperatures for the same year is provided.

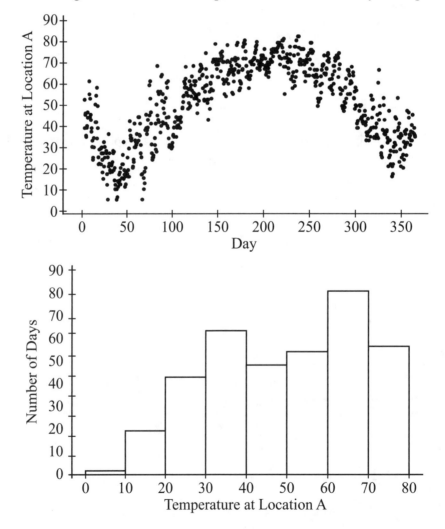

(a)   Give two facts that are obvious from the histogram but are not obvious from the time plot.

(b)   Give one fact that is obvious from the time plot but is not obvious from the histogram.

A time plot showing the temperatures at a different location, Location B, during the same year is shown below.

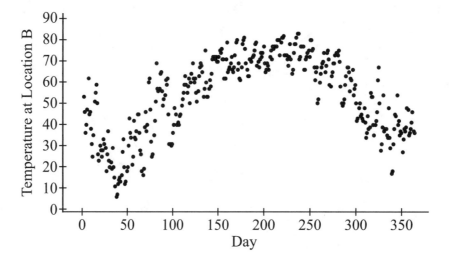

(c)   A scatterplot will be constructed where, for each day in the given year, the temperature at Location A will be plotted as the *x*-coordinate and the temperature at Location B will be plotted as the *y*-coordinate. Make a rough sketch as to what the appearance of this scatterplot would be. Include approximate scales on your axes, but do not attempt to plot points exactly.

(d)   Locations A and B are close geographically. A researcher wishes to establish whether, on average, the temperature at Location B is higher than at Location A. The researcher is willing to treat the days in the year considered above as a random sample of all days at the two locations. Name a hypothesis test that would be appropriate for answering the researcher's question.

The scatterplot below summarizes the temperatures at Location A and at a new location, Location C, for the days of the same year.

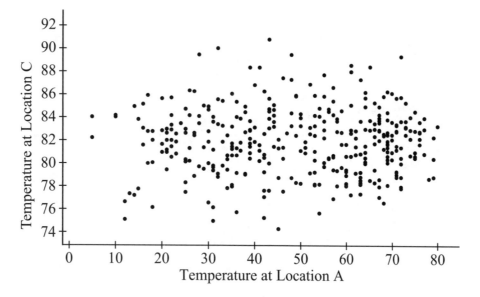

(e) Make a rough sketch of a possible appearance of the time plot for the temperatures at Location C during that same year. Include rough scales for your axes, but do not attempt to plot points exactly.

SAMPLE EXAMINATION FOUR
SECTION I

Time—1 hour and 30 minutes
Number of questions—40
Percent of total grade—50

Directions: Solve each of the following problems, using the available space for scratch work. Decide which is the best of the choices given and fill in the corresponding oval on the answer sheet. No credit will be given for anything written in the test book. Do not spend too much time on any one problem.

211

1. The dotplot below shows the number of goals scored by the Gator Girls soccer team in their games last year.

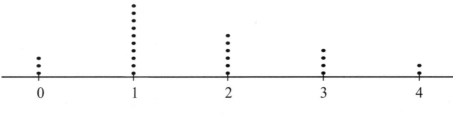

Number of Goals Scored

Which of the following could be used to compute the mean number of goals scored per game?

(A) $\dfrac{1+2}{2}$

(B) $\dfrac{0+1+2+3+4}{5}$

(C) $\dfrac{3+10+6+4+2}{5}$

(D) $\dfrac{3\cdot 0+10\cdot 1+6\cdot 2+4\cdot 3+2\cdot 4}{5}$

(E) $\dfrac{3\cdot 0+10\cdot 1+6\cdot 2+4\cdot 3+2\cdot 4}{3+10+6+4+2}$

Answer

2. There is concern that carrying weights while walking could increase the walker's blood pressure. In order to investigate this, an experiment is designed that will use a set of college student volunteers. None of the students has engaged in regular exercise prior to the experiment, and all of the students are willing to walk every day during the course of the experiment. By random assignment it is determined for each participant whether the person will carry in each hand weights of 2 pounds, 4 pounds, 6 pounds, or no weights at all, and <u>also</u> whether the person will walk 2 miles each day or 4 miles each day. The number of treatments used in this experiment is

(A) 1 (B) 2 (C) 4 (D) 6 (E) 8

Answer

3. In which of the following hypothesis tests could a t-distribution be the most appropriate distribution to use for calculation of the p-value?

(A) A test for a population mean where the population standard deviation is known
(B) A test for a population mean where the population standard deviation is unknown
(C) A test for a population proportion
(D) A goodness of fit test
(E) A test for independence of two categorical variables

Answer

4. Three brothers are arguing as to which of them did best in their end-of-year math exams. Robert, who is in the 10th grade, got an 84. Justin, who is in the 8th grade, got a 93. Bryan, who is in the 7th grade, got an 81. In order to sort out the argument, their mother suggests they ask their teachers what the overall means and standard deviations were for each of the exams. These quantities, along with the brothers' scores, are given in the table below.

	Score	Exam Mean	Exam Standard Deviation
Robert	84	77.1	7.3
Justin	93	82.0	7.8
Bryan	81	73.2	6.9

Using this information, the brothers decide which of them did best, which did second best, and which did third best, relative to their fellow students. Which of the following is the correct list (with the brother who did best relative to his fellow students first in the list)?

(A) Robert, Justin, Bryan
(B) Robert, Bryan, Justin
(C) Justin, Robert, Bryan
(D) Justin, Bryan, Robert
(E) Bryan, Robert, Justin

Answer

5. A large two-year college has found that the number of years completed by the population of students attending the college has the distribution given in the table below.

Number of Years Completed	0	1	2
Proportion of Students	0.08	0.22	0.70

(This tells us that 8% of students attending the college do not complete their first year, 22% complete their first year but not their second year, and the remaining 70% complete the entire two-year program.)

It can be calculated, using the information in the table, that the mean number of years completed for students attending this college is 1.62. Which of the following is the standard deviation of the number of years completed by students attending this college?

(A) $\sqrt{(0-1.62)^2 + (1-1.62)^2 + (2-1.62)^2}$

(B) $\sqrt{(0-1.62)^2(0.08) + (1-1.62)^2(0.22) + (2-1.62)^2(0.70)}$

(C) $\sqrt{\dfrac{(0-1.62)^2 + (1-1.62)^2 + (2-1.62)^2}{2}}$

(D) $\sqrt{\dfrac{(0-1.62)^2 + (1-1.62)^2 + (2-1.62)^2}{3}}$

(E) $\sqrt{\dfrac{(0-1.62)^2(0.08) + (1-1.62)^2(0.22) + (2-1.62)^2(0.70)}{3}}$

Answer

6. A researcher wishes to find out whether ducks of a particular breed tend to lay more eggs in the summer than in the winter. The researcher selects a random sample of ducks of this breed, and, over the course of a year, notes for each duck in the sample the number of eggs laid in the summer and the number of eggs laid in the winter. Which of the following would be a suitable test for analyzing the results of this study?

(A) One-sample z-test for a mean
(B) Two-sample t-test for means
(C) Paired t-test
(D) One-proportion z-test
(E) Two-proportion z-test

Answer

7. A large population has mean μ and standard deviation σ. A random sample of size n will be taken from the population. The Central Limit Theorem tells us that

(A) the mean of the sampling distribution of the sample mean is μ

(B) the standard deviation of the sampling distribution of the sample mean is $\dfrac{\sigma}{\sqrt{n}}$

(C) if n is large, the sampling distribution of the sample mean is approximately normal

(D) since the population is large, the sampling distribution of the sample mean must be approximately normal

(E) the standard deviation of the sampling distribution of the sample mean is greater than the standard deviation of the population

Answer

8. In a pilot study, a random sample of 98 adults is selected from a large town, and it is found that 33 of these 98 people consume vegetables three or more times per day. A one-proportion z-test is used to analyze this result. According to the test, does this sample result provide convincing evidence at a 5 percent level of significance that more than 25 percent of the adults in the town consume vegetables three or more times per day?

(A) Yes, since the test statistic is less than the critical value.
(B) Yes, since the test statistic is greater than the critical value.
(C) No, since the test statistic is less than the critical value.
(D) No, since the test statistic is greater than the critical value.
(E) The question cannot be answered, since the sample was not large enough for a one-proportion z-test to be used.

Answer

9. For two events A and B, let $P(A|B)$ denote the conditional probability that A occurs given that B occurs, and let $P(B|A)$ denote the conditional probability that B occurs given that A occurs. If $P(A \text{ and } B) \neq 0$, and $P(A|B) = P(B|A)$, which of the following must be true?

(A) A and B are independent.
(B) A and B are mutually exclusive.
(C) A and B have equal probabilities.
(D) The sum of the probabilities of A and B is 1.
(E) $P(A|B)$ and $P(B|A)$ are both equal to 1.

Answer

10.

Which of the following could be the value of the correlation coefficient for the data set represented by the scatterplot above?

(A) −0.91   (B) −0.34   (C) 0.03   (D) 0.34   (E) 0.91

Answer

11. Following an oil spill, a particular region of the ocean is being tested for the level of a chemical called naphthalene. It is considered fact that fish from the region will be safe to eat if, and only if, the mean naphthalene level in the region is less than 3.3 parts per billion. A set of water specimens will be randomly selected from the region and tested, and if the results provide convincing evidence that the mean naphthalene level is less than 3.3, then the sale of fish from the region will be made legal. Which of the following describes a Type I error and its consequences?

(A) The authorities obtain convincing evidence that the mean naphthalene level is less than 3.3, and legalize the sale of fish that are in fact <u>safe</u> for consumption.
(B) The authorities obtain convincing evidence that the mean naphthalene level is less than 3.3, and legalize the sale of fish that are in fact <u>unsafe</u> for consumption.
(C) The authorities fail to obtain convincing evidence that the mean naphthalene level is less than 3.3, and do not legalize the sale of fish from the region when in fact the fish are <u>safe</u> for consumption.
(D) The authorities fail to obtain convincing evidence that the mean naphthalene level is less than 3.3, and do not legalize the sale of fish from the region when in fact the fish are <u>unsafe</u> for consumption.
(E) The definition of a Type I error depends on the actual results of the study in question.

Answer

12. The cumulative relative frequency plot shown below summarizes the family earnings (expressed in US dollars) in a particular country. (The earnings of each family were expressed to the nearest dollar, and the cumulative relative frequencies in the graph indicate the proportions of families earning less than or equal to the amounts shown on the horizontal axis.)

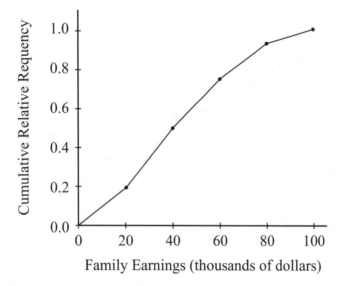

Which of the income brackets below contains the most families?

(A) $0 to $20,000
(B) $20,001 to $40,000
(C) $40,001 to $60,000
(D) $60,001 to $80,000
(E) $80,001 to $100,000

Answer

Questions 13 and 14 refer to the following scenario.

When a person watches a movie, does the video quality (how good the picture and sound are) make any difference as to how high the person rates the content of the movie? Suppose that 90 male college students are shown the same movie, watching in separate locations. By random assignment, 40 of the students are shown the movie in low video quality, with the other 50 students being shown the movie in high video quality. Each student is asked to rate the content of the movie as "Bad," "OK," or "Awesome." The results are shown in the table below.

		Rating of Content Quality			
		"Bad"	"OK"	"Awesome"	Total
Video Quality	Low	15	11	14	40
	High	14	12	24	50
	Total	29	23	38	90

A chi-square test for homogeneity will be used to analyze these results. The expected counts required for the test are shown in the table below.

		Rating of Content Quality			
		"Bad"	"OK"	"Awesome"	Total
Video Quality	Low	12.89	10.22	16.89	40
	High	16.11	12.78	21.11	50
	Total	29	23	38	90

13. Which of the following could be used to calculate the chi-square statistic for this hypothesis test?

(A) $\dfrac{40 \cdot 29}{90} + \dfrac{40 \cdot 23}{90} + \dfrac{40 \cdot 38}{90} + \dfrac{50 \cdot 29}{90} + \dfrac{50 \cdot 23}{90} + \dfrac{50 \cdot 38}{90}$

(B) $\dfrac{15 - 12.89}{15} + \dfrac{11 - 10.22}{11} + \dfrac{14 - 16.89}{14} + \dfrac{14 - 16.11}{14} + \dfrac{12 - 12.78}{12} + \dfrac{24 - 21.11}{24}$

(C) $\dfrac{|15 - 12.89|}{12.89} + \dfrac{|11 - 10.22|}{10.22} + \dfrac{|14 - 16.89|}{16.89} + \dfrac{|14 - 16.11|}{16.11} + \dfrac{|12 - 12.78|}{12.78} + \dfrac{|24 - 21.11|}{21.11}$

(D) $\dfrac{(15 - 12.89)^2}{15} + \dfrac{(11 - 10.22)^2}{11} + \dfrac{(14 - 16.89)^2}{14} + \dfrac{(14 - 16.11)^2}{14} + \dfrac{(12 - 12.78)^2}{12}$
$+ \dfrac{(24 - 21.11)^2}{24}$

(E) $\dfrac{(15 - 12.89)^2}{12.89} + \dfrac{(11 - 10.22)^2}{10.22} + \dfrac{(14 - 16.89)^2}{16.89} + \dfrac{(14 - 16.11)^2}{16.11} + \dfrac{(12 - 12.78)^2}{12.78}$

Answer

14. Of the following, which is closest to the true meaning of the *p*-value for this hypothesis test?

(A) The probability of getting observed counts that are at least as far from the expected counts as was the case in this study given that video quality has no effect on the rating of content quality

(B) The probability of getting observed counts that are at least as far from the expected counts as was the case in this study given that video quality has an effect on the rating of content quality

(C) The probability of getting the observed counts that were obtained in this study given that video quality has an effect on the rating of content quality

(D) The probability that video quality has no effect on the rating of content quality given the results that were obtained in this study

(E) The probability that video quality has an effect on the rating of content quality given the results that were obtained in this study

Answer

15. Tammi's high school consists of 840 students in grades 9–12. Tammi will select a simple random sample of 20 students from the school. Which of the following is NOT true?

(A) This could be achieved by printing the names of all 840 students on identical slips of paper, placing the slips in a large container, picking out 20 slips at random, and including in the sample the 20 students whose names are picked.

(B) This could be achieved by obtaining a list of the 840 students, assigning a distinct random 10-digit number to each student, sorting the list by the size of the random number, and including in the sample the first 20 names on the sorted list.

(C) Any subset of size 20 of the students at the school will have the same probability of being the sample that Tammi selects.

(D) Any student at the school will have the same probability of appearing in the sample.

(E) Tammi's method will ensure that there is an adequate representation of all four grades in the sample.

Answer

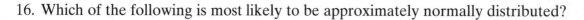

16. Which of the following is most likely to be approximately normally distributed?

(A) The scores on a very easy 5-question mental math quiz taken by a large number of students
(B) The scores on a large number of rolls of a cube whose faces are numbered 1 through 6
(C) The number of attempts it took to pass the drivers' test for the population of drivers in New York State
(D) The tail lengths of fully grown males of the common raccoon species
(E) The responses to a survey question given to a large number of people where the possible responses were "yes," "no," and "maybe"

Answer

17. A federation of play-based nursery and elementary schools has found, in the children at its schools, a correlation of 0.65 between time spent playing with brick-based construction toys in nursery school (in minutes per day) and first grade math score (on a scale of 0 to 100). Which of the following is implied by this information?

(A) Playing with brick-based construction toys in nursery school causes an increase in first grade math score.
(B) If the time spent playing with brick-based construction toys had been recorded in hours per day instead of minutes per day, then the correlation would have been 0.65/60.
(C) When time spent playing with brick-based construction toys (in minutes per day) increases by 1, the average increase in first grade math score is 0.65.
(D) If two children are selected from those included in the study, then the one with the greater time spent playing with brick-based construction toys will have the higher first grade math score.
(E) Less than half of the variation in first grade math score can be explained by the regression line of first grade math score on time spent playing with brick-based construction toys in nursery school.

Answer

18. When an experiment is intended to compare two or more treatments, a good design <u>must</u>

   (A) include a control group
   (B) include some random assignment to treatments
   (C) include a group that receives a placebo
   (D) involve some sort of blocking
   (E) be double blind

Answer

19. Which of the following is/are true?

   I. In a *t*-test for a single population mean, increasing the sample size (while leaving everything else the same) changes the number of degrees of freedom used in the test.

   II. In a chi-square test for independence, increasing the sample size (while leaving everything else the same) changes the number of degrees of freedom used in the test.

   III. In a *t*-test for the slope of the population regression line, increasing the number of observations (while leaving everything else the same) changes the number of degrees of freedom used in the test.

   (A) I only
   (B) I and II only
   (C) I and III only
   (D) II and III only
   (E) I, II and III

Answer

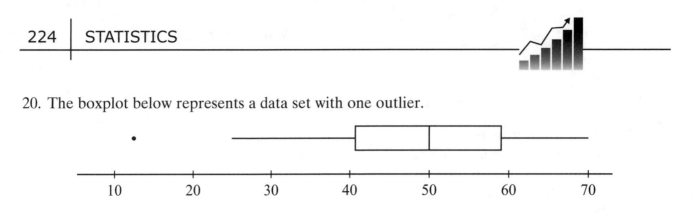

20. The boxplot below represents a data set with one outlier.

If the outlier were to be removed, what would happen to the mean and the standard deviation of the data set?

(A) Both the mean and the standard deviation would remain the same.
(B) Both the mean and the standard deviation would increase.
(C) Both the mean and the standard deviation would decrease.
(D) The mean would increase and the standard deviation would decrease.
(E) The mean would decrease and the standard deviation would increase.

Answer

21. A town has recently moved over to single stream recycling, an approach to waste disposal that recycles a far greater proportion of household refuse than the town's previous approach. Local administrators are interested in determining the degree to which the new approach is being adopted by households in the town. Of the following, which would be likely to produce the most accurate answer to the administrators' question?

(A) Placing researchers at the town's Whole Nutrition food market, and having the researchers select customers of varying genders and ethnicities. The researchers ask the people to state whether they "strongly agree," "agree," "have no opinion," "disagree" or "strongly disagree" with the statement: "My household has substantially changed its approach to refuse disposal as a result of the town's recent change."

(B) Placing researchers at the town's railroad station, bus terminal, mall, and supermarkets, and having the researchers select people of varying genders, ethnicities, and socioeconomic backgrounds. The researchers ask the people to state whether they "strongly agree," "agree," "have no opinion," "disagree" or "strongly disagree" with the statement: "My household has substantially changed its approach to refuse disposal as a result of the town's policies of improving the environment by recycling greater proportions of household waste."

(C) Selecting a large random sample from a complete list of households. Telephone or visit the households selected (repeatedly returning until a response is obtained) asking an adult to state whether he/she "strongly agrees," "agrees," "has no opinion," "disagrees" or "strongly disagrees" with the statement: "My household has substantially changed its approach to refuse disposal as a result of the town's recent change."

(D) Placing leaflets in the mailboxes of all the households in the town asking an adult from the household to respond online to a survey. The online survey asks people to state whether they "strongly agree," "agree," "have no opinion," "disagree" or "strongly disagree" with the statement: "My household has substantially changed its approach to refuse disposal as a result of the town's recent change."

(E) Scheduling a phone-in program on the local radio station that discusses people's feelings and impressions regarding the town's recent change of policy.

Answer

22. Let the proportion of houses in a large city that have mold in their basements be p. When a random sample of n houses is selected from the city, which of the following is the standard deviation of the sampling distribution of $\hat{p}$, the proportion of houses in the sample that have mold in their basements?

(A) $\sqrt{\dfrac{p(1-p)}{n}}$

(B) $\sqrt{\dfrac{\hat{p}(1-\hat{p})}{n}}$

(C) $\dfrac{\hat{p}(1-\hat{p})}{n}$

(D) $\sqrt{np(1-p)}$

(E) $\sqrt{n\hat{p}(1-\hat{p})}$

Answer

23. Jimmy, a very promising 8th grader, is taking an AP Statistics class. The teacher has generated on a computer a large set of numbers that are approximately normally distributed and are being considered as the population. Each student is asked to select a random sample from the population and use the sample to construct a 95% confidence interval for the population mean. Jimmy goes ahead and does this. However, when the teacher announces the true population mean to the class, Jimmy notices that the population mean does not lie within his confidence interval. Which of the following is true?

(A) Jimmy's work could have been correct. Confidence intervals are designed to be narrow, and therefore, for most random samples, the population parameter being estimated will not lie within the interval.

(B) Jimmy's work could have been correct. For about 5% of students doing this exercise correctly the population mean will not lie within the confidence interval calculated.

(C) Jimmy's work could have been correct. It will always be the case that the population mean is not within the confidence interval when the population mean doesn't happen to be in the sample selected.

(D) There must be an error in Jimmy's work. The whole point of confidence intervals is that they should capture the population parameter that is being estimated.

(E) There must be an error in Jimmy's work. He must have calculated an interval that was too narrow, and it was this that caused the interval not to capture the population mean.

Answer

24. Suppose that a detailed study has revealed that for romance novels the number of pages has mean 364 and standard deviation 47, and that for detective novels the number of pages has mean 404 and standard deviation 173. A reader is going to select at random one romance novel, independently select at random one detective novel, and read both books. What is the standard deviation of the total number of pages the person will read?

(A) 14.8 (B) 110.0 (C) 179.3 (D) 220.0 (E) 321.4

Answer

25. The management of a relatively new social networking website named BooglePlus is conducting a pilot study comparing use of its own site with use of a longer established social networking site named FaceList. Some articles published on the Internet give the reader the opportunity to register votes (called "likes") for the article on social networking sites to which the reader belongs. A BooglePlus employee selects from the Internet a random sample of 28 articles where the opportunity is given for registering votes for the article on both BooglePlus and FaceList. Letting x be the number of votes on FaceList and y be the number of votes on the BooglePlus, the slope of the least squares regression line of y on x is found to be 0.0623, with a standard error of 0.0224. Which of the following could be used to compute a 95% confidence interval for the slope of the population regression line of y on x?

(A) $0.0623 \pm (2.056)(0.0224)$
(B) $0.0623 \pm (2.052)(0.0224)$
(C) $0.0623 \pm (2.048)(0.0224)$
(D) $0.0224 \pm (2.056)(0.0623)$
(E) $0.0224 \pm (2.052)(0.0623)$

Answer

26. The housing units on a street have been categorized as to their type ("house" or "apartment") and occupants ("single adult," "couple only," or "with children"). The results are shown in the table below.

		Occupants			
		Single Adult	Couple Only	With Children	Total
Type of Housing Unit	House	5	14	28	47
	Apartment	25	28	20	73
	Total	30	42	48	120

Which of the following is true?

(A) There are more houses than apartments on this street.

(B) More than half of the housing units contain children.

(C) Of the three occupants categories the one with the highest proportion of apartments is "couples only."

(D) Of the two types of housing unit the one with the higher proportion categorized as "couples only" is apartments.

(E) The proportion of houses that contain couples only is smaller than the proportion of apartments that contain children.

Answer

27. A particular scale of personality was designed so that, in the country where it was formulated, the distribution of scores for the whole country was approximately normal, with mean 100 and standard deviation 15. Which of the following events is most likely?

(A) The mean personality score for a random sample of 9 people from the country is between 95 and 105

(B) The mean personality score for a random sample of 9 people from the country is between 90 and 110

(C) The mean personality score for a random sample of 16 people from the country is between 98 and 102

(D) The mean personality score for a random sample of 16 people from the country is between 95 and 105

(E) The mean personality score for a random sample of 16 people from the country is between 90 and 110

Answer

28. A computer contains on its hard drive 464 spreadsheet files. The sizes of these files, in kilobytes (KB), are summarized in the histogram below.

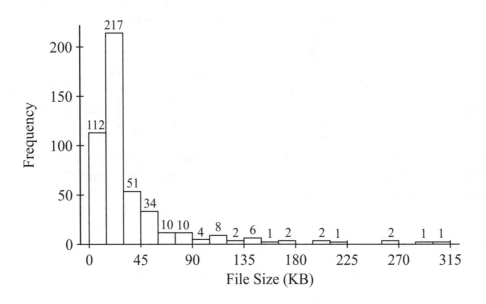

Which of the following is true about the distribution of file sizes?

(A) The median is greater than 30.
(B) The range is greater than 320.
(C) The first quartile is less than 15.
(D) The interquartile range is less than 30.
(E) The distribution is negatively skewed.

Answer

29. A company is comparing the use of two different robots for the detection of contaminants in river water. A random sample of 10 river locations is selected, and Robot 1 is used to locate a particular contaminant at those locations. Then a random sample of 15 further river locations is independently selected, and Robot 2 is used to locate the same contaminant at these locations. The sample means and standard deviations of the times taken (in minutes) to locate the contaminant are given in the table below.

	Sample Size	Mean	Standard Deviation
Robot 1	10	2.886	0.525
Robot 2	15	3.114	0.644

A two-sample *t*-test will be used to determine whether the results provide convincing evidence of a difference between the population mean times to locate the contaminant. Which of the following correctly calculates the test statistic?

(A) $\dfrac{2.886 - 3.114}{\sqrt{\dfrac{0.525}{10} + \dfrac{0.644}{15}}}$

(B) $\dfrac{2.886 - 3.114}{\sqrt{\dfrac{0.525}{9} + \dfrac{0.644}{14}}}$

(C) $\dfrac{2.886 - 3.114}{\sqrt{\dfrac{(0.525)^2}{10} + \dfrac{(0.644)^2}{15}}}$

(D) $\dfrac{2.886 - 3.114}{\sqrt{\dfrac{(0.525)^2}{9} + \dfrac{(0.644)^2}{14}}}$

(E) $\dfrac{2.886 - 3.114}{\sqrt{\left(\dfrac{0.525 + 0.644}{2}\right)\left(\dfrac{1}{10} + \dfrac{1}{15}\right)}}$

Answer

30. A small class consists of 8 girls and 4 boys. If a team of 4 students is selected at random, what is the probability that all the students on the team are girls?

(A) 0.141   (B) 0.198   (C) 0.255   (D) 0.312   (E) 0.369

Answer

31. A hypothesis test of the null hypothesis H_0 *versus* the alternative hypothesis H_a is performed, using a significance level of α. If the *p*-value for the test is greater than α, which of the following is a correct conclusion to the test?

(A) H_0 is accepted. We have convincing evidence that H_a is false.
(B) H_0 is not rejected. We do not have convincing evidence that H_a is true.
(C) H_0 is not rejected. We have convincing evidence that H_a is false.
(D) H_0 is rejected. We have convincing evidence that H_a is true.
(E) H_0 is rejected. We do not have convincing evidence that H_a is false.

Answer

Questions 32 and 33 refer to the following scenario.

A study using satellites recorded the mass of ice and the number of lightning flashes per minute in thunderstorm cells over a particular region of the country. Prior to analyzing the data, the researchers transformed both variables using logarithms (base 10). They then performed a linear regression of $\log(y)$ on $\log(x)$, where x = ice mass (in kg) and y = number of lightning flashes per minute.

32. The least squares regression line of $\log(y)$ on $\log(x)$ resulting from the regression analysis was

$$\text{predicted value of } \log(y) = -0.285 + 0.2255 \log(x).$$

What does the model predict for the number of lightning flashes per minute when the ice mass is 66,000,000 kg?

(A) 2.1   (B) 5.9   (C) 16.8   (D) 23.8   (E) 30.1

Answer

33. A regression analysis produced the following residual plot.

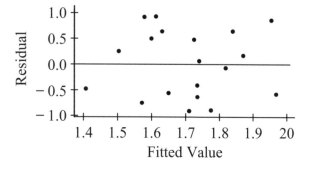

Fitted Value

According to the residual plot, does a linear regression appear to be appropriate for modeling the relationship between the transformed variables?

(A) Yes, because the residual plot shows a random pattern.
(B) Yes, because the vertical spread of points in the residual plot is roughly centered about the horizontal axis that represents a zero residual.
(C) No, because there is no sign of a clear curve in the residual plot.
(D) No, because the best fit line in the residual plot is roughly horizontal.
(E) No, because logarithms base 10 were used, when natural logarithms are more appropriate for use with physical data.

Answer

34. When two cubes, each with faces numbered 1 through 6, are rolled, what is the probability that the total score is 11?

(A) $\frac{1}{36}$ (B) $\frac{1}{24}$ (C) $\frac{1}{18}$ (D) $\frac{1}{12}$ (E) $\frac{1}{6}$

Answer

35. There are large numbers of jobs available in Town A and in Town B. A researcher selects a sample of 97 jobs available in Town A and a sample of 94 jobs available in Town B. The salaries offered for the jobs in the samples are noted, and the results will used to construct a confidence interval for $\mu_A - \mu_B$, where μ_A is the mean salary for all jobs available in Town A and μ_B is the mean salary for all jobs available in Town B. Which of the following is NOT true about construction of the confidence interval, and the interval that is obtained?

(A) It is necessary to assume that the samples are independent and random.
(B) It is necessary to assume that the population distributions are normal.
(C) A t-distribution could be used.
(D) The quantity $\overline{x}_A - \overline{x}_B$ will lie at the center of the interval, where $\overline{x}_A$ and $\overline{x}_B$ are the sample means for Town A and Town B, respectively.
(E) If larger samples had been used, then the confidence interval would probably have been narrower.

Answer

36. A student at a kindergarten-through-12th-grade private school takes a sample of students at the school, and finds, amongst the students in the sample, a positive association between the sizes of their feet and how fast they can run. The student concludes, "All other things being equal, if you want a faster runner you should probably choose someone with large feet." A teacher responds, "That doesn't follow! Kids with bigger feet tend to be older, and older kids tend to be faster runners. For students of the same age, running speed might have nothing to do with foot size!" Which of the following is being considered a confounding variable in this context?

(A) Method of sampling
(B) Method of measuring running speed
(C) Foot size
(D) Age
(E) Running speed

Answer

37. The masses of the berries produced by a particular type of tree can be assumed to be normally distributed with a standard deviation of 72 milligrams. If a berry of this type is selected at random, which of the following represents the probability that the mass of the berry is within 54 milligrams of the mean mass of berries of this type?

(A) $P(z < 0.75)$
(B) $P(z < -0.75)$
(C) $P(z > 0.75)$
(D) $P(z < -0.75) + P(z > 0.75)$
(E) $P(z < 0.75) - P(z < -0.75)$

Answer

38. A simple random sample is selected from a population, and a measurement is taken for each individual in the sample. Using these results, the 95% confidence interval for the population mean is found to be (58.770, 61.428). (The conditions for construction of the interval were checked and verified.) The results from the same sample are now to be used to perform a hypothesis test. If a significance level of $\alpha = 0.05$ is used, which of the following is true?

(A) In a test of $H_0: \mu = 57$ against $H_a: \mu \neq 57$, H_0 would be rejected.
(B) In a test of $H_0: \mu = 57$ against $H_a: \mu < 57$, H_0 would be rejected.
(C) In a test of $H_0: \mu = 59$ against $H_a: \mu \neq 59$, H_0 would be rejected.
(D) In a test of $H_0: \mu = 60$ against $H_a: \mu > 60$, H_0 would be rejected.
(E) In a test of $H_0: \mu = 62$ against $H_a: \mu < 62$, H_0 would not be rejected.

Answer

39. Forty volunteers have been gathered as subjects in an experiment to compare two treatments. These experimental subjects will be randomly assigned to two groups, each of size 20. Random assignment to the groups ensures that

(A) the groups are exactly the same with respect to any variable that might have an effect on a person's response to either of the treatments
(B) any initial differences between the people in the two groups occur completely by chance
(C) the results of the experiment will be the same for the two groups
(D) the participants won't know which treatment they are receiving
(E) the people will not be in the same group as their friends

Answer

40. In which of the following scenarios could a two-proportion z-test be used for the hypothesis test mentioned? (In the scenario or scenarios where the two-proportion z-test is appropriate, you may assume that the conditions for use of the test are met.)

   I. A random sample of adults is selected from Neighborhood A and an independent random sample of adults is selected from Neighborhood B. Each adult selected is asked this question: "If you're shopping in a supermarket and the total bill is between $10 and $20, do you prefer to pay using cash or some other method?" A hypothesis test is used to compare the proportions of adults in the two neighbor hoods responding that they would use cash.

   II. A random sample of adults is selected from Neighborhood A and an independent random sample of adults is selected from Neighborhood B. Each adult selected is asked this question: "If you're shopping in a supermarket and the total bill is between $10 and $20, do you prefer to pay using cash, a debit card, or a credit card?" A hypothesis test is used to compare the proportions of adults falling into the three categories for the two neighborhoods.

   III. The cashiers at a supermarket are given instructions as to how to randomly assign each customer (without the customer knowing) to either Group A or Group B. Customers assigned to Group A will be asked "Would you like to use cash or a card for your payment?" Customers assigned to Group B will be asked "Would you like to use a card or cash for your payment?" A hypothesis test is used to compare the proportions of customers in the two groups who choose to use cash.

(A) I only
(B) II only
(C) I and II
(D) I and III
(E) II and III

Answer

SECTION II PART A

Questions 1–5
Spend about 65 minutes on this part of the exam.
Percent of Section II grade—75

Directions: Show all your work. Indicate clearly the methods you use, because you will be graded on the correctness of your method as well as on the accuracy and completeness of your results and explanations.

1. An experiment was conducted to compare the influence of an adult of the same sex with that of an adult of the opposite sex in terms of nurturing behavior in children. The experiment used 72 nursery school children aged 3 to 6, and the children were randomly assigned to three groups, with 24 children in each group.

   In the first group, named the "Same-sex adult" group, each child was placed in a room along with some appealing activities such as colored pens and blank coloring books. At the same time, an adult of the same sex as the child was seated in another part of the room with various items including some furry toys. For 10 minutes, the adult showed strong nurturing behavior toward the furry toys while the child played in the other part of the room. Then, for 20 minutes, the child was given unsupervised access to same items as those the adult had used, including the furry toys. During this time the child was observed, and the number of nurturing acts shown towards the furry toys by the child was noted.

   The children in the second group, the "Different-sex adult" group, were given the same treatment as those in the first group, except that the adult model was of the opposite sex to that of the child. Each child's behavior was measured in the same way as in first group.

   Children in the third group, the control group, were given the same treatment, except that the adult involved did not show nurturing behavior towards the toys. (In this group, the sex of the adult was chosen randomly.) Each child's behavior was measured in the same way as in the first two groups.

   The results of the experiment are summarized in the boxplots below.

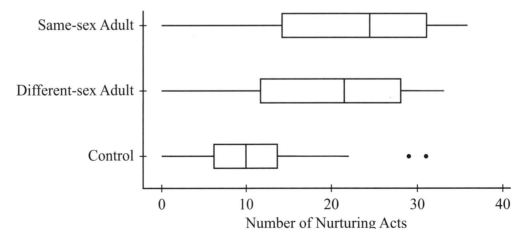

(a)   Compare the distributions of the number of nurturing acts among the three groups.

(b)   For the "Same-sex adult" group, would the mean most likely have been greater than the median, or less than the median? Explain how you reach your conclusion.

(c)   How was the design of this experiment improved by the inclusion of a control group?

2. A consumer organization compared the screen sizes and prices of fourteen global positioning system (GPS) units. The fourteen GPS units used in the study included units with screen sizes as small as 3.5 inches and as large as 7 inches. Prices ranged between $90 and $230. Some computer output from a regression analysis of these data is shown below.

```
Predictor         Coef        StDev         T            P
Constant         -9.47        29.65       -0.32        0.755
Screen size     32.461        6.777        4.79        0.000

S = 22.3293      R-Sq = 65.7%     R-Sq(adj) = 62.8%
```

(a) Using the computer output, write the equation of the least squares regression line that describes the relationship between price and screen size.

(b) Suppose that two GPS units are selected, and the screen sizes of the two units differ by 4 inches. According to the least squares regression line, how much more than the unit with the smaller screen is the one with the larger screen expected to cost?

(c)   What does the least squares regression line predict for the price of a GPS unit whose screen size is 6.5 inches?

A scatterplot for this data set, including the least squares regression line, is shown below.

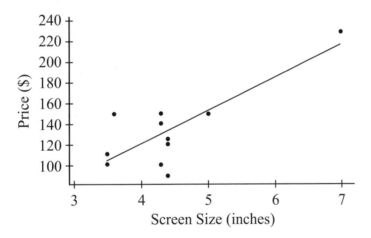

(d)   Suppose that the GPS unit with a screen size of 7 inches were to be removed from the data set. Would the line shown in the scatterplot provide the best description of the relationship for the remaining data values? Why, or why not?

3. A study conducted at a large hospital found that 27.8 percent of all patients admitted to the hospital's intensive care unit (ICU) remained in the ICU for less than 24 hours.

(a) If 8 patients are selected at random from the ICU patients at this hospital, what is the probability that 2 or fewer of them remained in the ICU for less than 24 hours?

(b) Suppose that 20 patients are selected at random from the ICU patients at this hospital. Calculate the mean and the standard deviation of the number of these patients who remained in the ICU for less than 24 hours.

(c) Another result of the study was that for elective (non-emergency) admissions to the hospital's ICU, the length of stay in the ICU had a mean of 18.9 hours and a standard deviation of 3.9 hours. Assuming that the length of stay in the ICU for elective admissions is approximately normally distributed, what proportion of elective admissions remained in the ICU for less than 24 hours?

4. The current inventory of a library consists of 198,233 items. The items are categorized as journals, books, DVDs, and other media. The numbers of items falling into the four categories are given in the table below.

Category	Journals	Books	DVDs	Other
Number of Items	124327	56340	10469	7097

(a) Complete the table below showing the proportions of the entire inventory falling into the given categories.

Category	Journals	Books	DVDs	Other
Proportion of Inventory		0.284		

(b) The chief librarian is preparing a report regarding the patterns of use of the library. To assist with this, a coworker compiles data regarding library use during the previous week. The numbers of items used in the four categories during that week are shown in the table below.

Category	Journals	Books	DVDs	Other
Number of Items Used	600	353	58	30

The librarians are willing to treat the uses of the library during that week as a random sample from the set of all uses of the library. Do these results provide convincing evidence that the proportions of all uses that fall into the four categories are different from the proportions of items in those categories (the numbers in the table in part (a))? Provide statistical evidence to support your answer.

5. A student who is writing an article about music for the school newspaper asks another student, Chin-Sun, to estimate the mean length of the mp3 downloads available on a particular web site. Being an AP Statistics student, Chin-Sun decides to make this estimate using a confidence interval. She randomly selects 15 songs from the site, and makes note of their lengths in seconds. Chin-Sun then uses these results to construct a 95% confidence interval for the mean length of all songs on the site. Prior to gathering this sample, Chin-Sun has no knowledge of the lengths of the songs on the site.

(a) In order to find the critical value to use in the calculation of her confidence interval, should Chin-Sun use the standard normal (z) distribution or a t distribution? Explain your answer.

(b) What is the meaning of 95% confidence in this context?

(c)   Using the results from her sample, Chin-Sun checks and verifies all the conditions for inference, and correctly calculates the confidence interval for the mean length (in seconds) of all songs on the site to be 242.733 ± 19.209. What was the standard deviation of the song lengths in Chin-Sun's sample?

SECTION II PART B

Question 6
Spend about 25 minutes on this part of the exam.
Percent of Section II grade—25

Directions: Show all your work. Indicate clearly the methods you use, because you will be graded on the correctness of your method as well as on the accuracy and completeness of your results and explanations.

6. The owner of a small company is planning an economic impact study that will include information about local spending by the company's employees. Spending information is gathered by means of a detailed survey, and so the owner initially plans to select a simple random sample of 8 employees, and require only those 8 people to complete the survey. The company has 32 employees in total.

   (a)   Explain how the simple random sample of 8 employees might be selected.

The company's 32 employees are paid at three grade levels: 16 at the "Individual Contributor" level, 12 at the "Professional" level, and 4 at the "Managerial" level. A statistician advising the owner suggests use of a stratified random sample consisting of 4 individual contributors, 3 professionals, and 1 manager.

(b)   Why would it be sensible, for the purposes of this study, to stratify by employee grade level?

The economic impact study will include an estimate of the mean local spending for the 32 employees of the company. The statistician wishes to explain further the benefit of using the stratified sampling method described above for estimation of this mean. In order to do this, the statistician creates a list of hypothetical annual local spending values for all 32 employees. These values (in thousands of dollars, rounded to the nearest one-thousand), along with the employees' grade levels, are shown in the table on the next page. (The employees have been sorted according to their hypothetical annual spending values.)

Employee Number	Grade Level	Hypothetical Annual Spending (in thousands of dollars)
5	Individual	9
1	Individual	10
3	Individual	11
2	Individual	13
4	Individual	13
11	Individual	13
14	Individual	13
9	Individual	14
16	Individual	14
6	Individual	15
10	Individual	15
13	Individual	15
23	Professional	15
24	Professional	15
7	Individual	17
8	Individual	17
12	Individual	17
28	Professional	17
15	Individual	18
18	Professional	18
19	Professional	18
20	Professional	18
17	Professional	19
25	Professional	19
26	Professional	19
27	Professional	19
21	Professional	20
22	Professional	20
30	Managerial	20
29	Managerial	22
32	Managerial	22
31	Managerial	26

Suppose that a simple random sample of 8 employees is used for the study, and that the hypothetical spending values given in the table are true. Then the smallest possible sample mean for the 8 employees selected is given by

$$\overline{x}_{min} = \frac{9 + 10 + 11 + 13 + 13 + 13 + 13 + 14}{8} = 12,$$

and the largest possible sample mean is given by

$$\overline{x}_{max} = \frac{19 + 19 + 20 + 20 + 20 + 22 + 22 + 26}{8} = 21.$$

(c) Suppose, now, that the stratified sampling method described before part (b) is used. Assuming that the spending values given in the table are true, find the smallest and largest possible values of the sample mean, and add your values to the number line given. (The number line also shows the mean hypothetical spending for all employees, which is 17.5.)

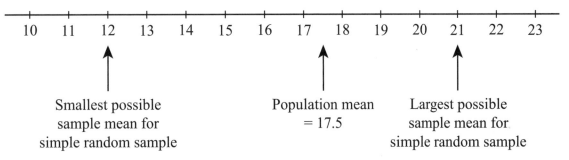

(d)   The answer to part (c) suggests that one of the two sampling methods produces a sample mean that has a smaller variability than the sample mean produced by the other sampling method. Which of the two sampling methods is this? Explain how you reach your conclusion.

(e)   It is known that, over all possible samples, the two sampling methods will both produce sample means that are, on average, equal to the population mean of 17.5. Use your answer to part (d) to explain why, for estimation of the population mean, the stratified random sampling described here would be preferable to simple random sampling.

SAMPLE EXAMINATION FIVE
SECTION I

Time—1 hour and 30 minutes
Number of questions—40
Percent of total grade—50

Directions: Solve each of the following problems, using the available space for scratch work. Decide which is the best of the choices given and fill in the corresponding oval on the answer sheet. No credit will be given for anything written in the test book. Do not spend too much time on any one problem.

1. A company has recently given some pay raises. The distribution of the amounts by which the employees' salaries have been increased is illustrated by the boxplot below.

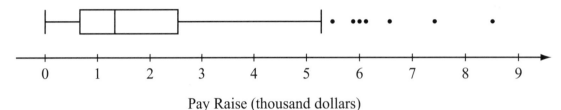

Pay Raise (thousand dollars)

Which of the following best describes the shape of the distribution and the interquartile range (IQR) of the salary increases?

(A) symmetrical; IQR is approximately $700
(B) skewed to the right; IQR is approximately $700
(C) skewed to the left; IQR is approximately $700
(D) skewed to the right; IQR is approximately $2000
(E) skewed to the left; IQR is approximately $2000

Answer

2. A researcher is studying an old edition of an encyclopedia. She wishes to estimate the proportion of the printed matter in the encyclopedia that is diagrams and pictures (as opposed to text). The encyclopedia consists of 30 volumes, and she observes that the proportion of printed matter that is diagrams and pictures is roughly the same in each of the volumes. The researcher randomly selects four of the volumes, and then studies every page in those four volumes. This is an example of which type of sampling?

(A) Cluster
(B) Convenience
(C) Simple random
(D) Stratified random
(E) Systematic

Answer

3. A company produces cloth for use in airplane seats. The company claims that the mean breaking strength μ for specimens of the cloth is 80 pounds of force, but the airlines who buy the cloth are concerned that the cloth might be weaker than that. A group working on behalf of the airlines takes a random sample of specimens of the cloth and finds the breaking strength of each specimen in the sample. What hypotheses should the group use to test the manufacturer's claim?

(A) $H_0: \mu = 80$, $H_a: \mu < 80$

(B) $H_0: \mu = 80$, $H_a: \mu \neq 80$

(C) $H_0: \mu = 80$, $H_a: \mu > 80$

(D) $H_0: \mu < 80$, $H_a: \mu = 80$

(E) $H_0: \mu > 80$, $H_a: \mu = 80$

Answer

4. In a company, 78% of the employees opt for medical insurance and 42% of the employees opt for life insurance. 82% of the employees opt for at least one of these benefits. What percent of the employees opt for both of these benefits?

(A) 4%   (B) 18%   (C) 33%   (D) 38%   (E) 40%

Answer

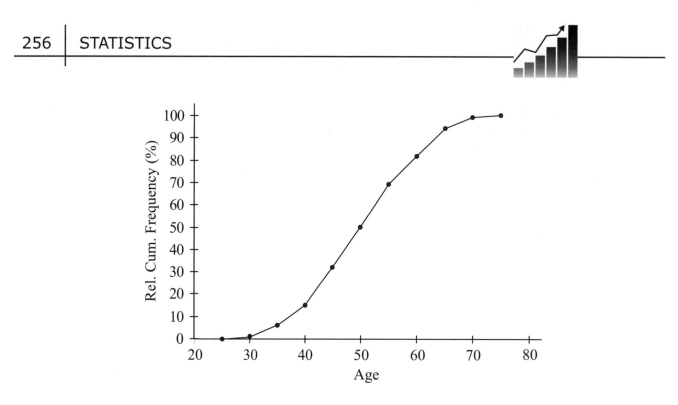

5. A society has 160 members. A relative cumulative frequency graph of their ages is shown in the figure above. Approximately how many of the society's members are over 43 years old?

(A) 25   (B) 40   (C) 48   (D) 75   (E) 120

Answer

6. A track and field coach wants to find out whether a particular hammer thrower performs better, on average, in the morning or in the afternoon. The coach observes a random sample of the athlete's morning throws and a random sample of the athlete's afternoon throws. Which one of the following significance tests could be used to analyze the results?

(A) One-sample t-test for a mean
(B) Two-sample t-test for means
(C) Paired t-test
(D) One-proportion z-test
(E) Two-proportion z-test

Answer

7. Diana has several children and each of her children has several friends, so she can never be sure how many children will come to dinner. However, over long experience she has worked out that the probability distribution for the number of children who will come to dinner is as shown below.

Number of children	0	1	2	3	4	5	6	7	8	9	10
Probability	0.01	0.04	0.13	0.15	0.16	0.17	0.12	0.09	0.07	0.04	0.02

On any given evening, what is the minimum number of places that she should set at the dinner table for the children in order to be at least 80% sure that all the children can be seated?

(A) 6   (B) 7   (C) 8   (D) 9   (E) 10

Answer

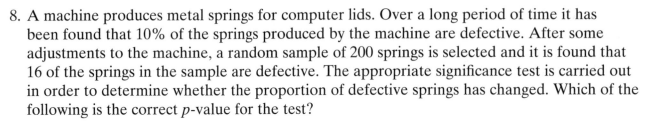

8. A machine produces metal springs for computer lids. Over a long period of time it has been found that 10% of the springs produced by the machine are defective. After some adjustments to the machine, a random sample of 200 springs is selected and it is found that 16 of the springs in the sample are defective. The appropriate significance test is carried out in order to determine whether the proportion of defective springs has changed. Which of the following is the correct p-value for the test?

(A) $2 \cdot P\left(z < \dfrac{0.08 - 0.1}{\sqrt{\dfrac{(0.1)(0.9)}{200}}}\right)$

(B) $2 \cdot P\left(z > \dfrac{0.08 - 0.1}{\sqrt{\dfrac{(0.1)(0.9)}{200}}}\right)$

(C) $2 \cdot P\left(z < \dfrac{0.08 - 0.1}{\sqrt{\dfrac{(.08)(.92)}{200}}}\right)$

(D) $2 \cdot P\left(z > \dfrac{0.08 - 0.1}{\sqrt{\dfrac{(.08)(.92)}{200}}}\right)$

(E) $\dfrac{1}{2} \cdot P\left(z < \dfrac{0.08 - 0.1}{\sqrt{\dfrac{(.08)(.92)}{200}}}\right)$

Answer

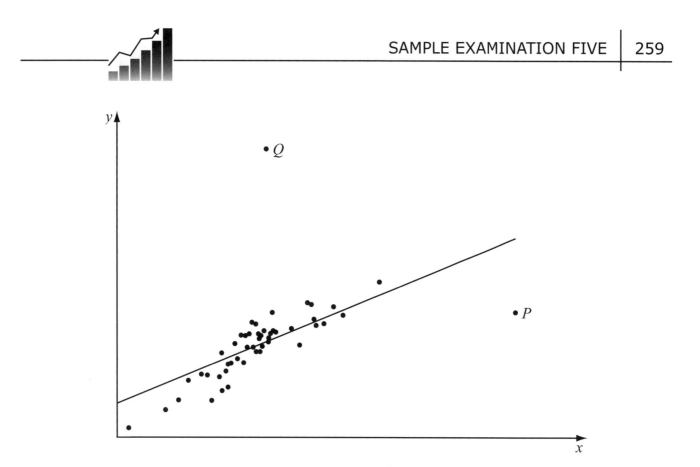

9. The scatterplot above shows 52 points with the associated least squares regression line for predicting values of y from values of x. One of the two labeled points – either P or Q – will be removed. Which of the following is true?

(A) Removal of the point P would substantially increase the slope of the least squares regression line. Removal of the point Q would have little effect on the slope of the least squares regression line.

(B) Removal of the point P would substantially decrease the slope of the least squares regression line. Removal of the point Q would have little effect on the slope of the least squares regression line.

(C) Removal of the point Q would substantially increase the slope of the least squares regression line. Removal of the point P would have little effect on the slope of the least squares regression line.

(D) Removal of the point Q would substantially decrease the slope of the least squares regression line. Removal of the point P would have little effect on the slope of the least squares regression line.

(E) Removal of the point P would have a substantial effect on the slope of the least squares regression line <u>and</u> removal of the point Q would have a substantial effect on the slope of the least squares regression line.

Answer

10. In a particular country it is known that 40% of the residents have blue eyes, 35% of the residents have brown eyes, and 25% of the residents have green eyes. A student carries out a study to determine whether, in terms of color, the eyes of dolls manufactured in that country are representative of the residents of the country. The student takes a random sample of 40 brands of doll, and finds that 10 of them have blue eyes, 19 of them have brown eyes, and 11 of them have green eyes. She then carries out the appropriate significance test and obtains the p-value for the test. Which of the following is true?

(A) The p-value is between 0 and 0.05.
(B) The p-value is between 0.05 and 0.1.
(C) The p-value is between 0.1 and 0.15.
(D) The p-value is between 0.15 and 0.2.
(E) The p-value is greater than 0.2.

Answer

11. When Joe plays a board game with his four sisters, any one of the five players is equally likely to win. They decide to play the game repeatedly until Joe wins a game, and then they will stop. Assuming that the outcomes of the games are independent, what is the probability that they play at least three games?

(A) 0.128   (B) 0.312   (C) 0.488   (D) 0.512   (E) 0.640

Answer

12. A vending machine delivers varying amounts of coffee. The standard deviation of the amount per serving is known, but the mean amount per serving has recently been adjusted to an unknown value. The person responsible for the machine takes ten servings of coffee from the machine, and is willing to assume that these ten servings form a random sample. She calculates the sample mean serving size to be 10.8 ounces.

She now intends to carry out a z-test about the mean serving size μ for all servings of coffee from this machine. Which of the following pairs of hypotheses will result in the smallest p-value?

(A) $H_0: \mu = 10$, $H_a: \mu < 10$

(B) $H_0: \mu = 10$, $H_a: \mu > 10$

(C) $H_0: \mu = 11$, $H_a: \mu < 11$

(D) $H_0: \mu = 11$, $H_a: \mu \neq 11$

(E) $H_0: \mu = 11$, $H_a: \mu > 11$

Answer

13. A student named Russell does a survey concerning the amount of sleep his fellow students are getting. Having taken a sample of students and asked each student the total amount of sleep he/she has had over the past week, he discovers that one of the responses is an outlier. Russell strongly suspects that this response was untrue, but he does not feel able to exclude it from his data set. In order to summarize the center and the spread of the complete set of responses he should quote the

(A) mean and the standard deviation
(B) mean and the interquartile range
(C) mean and the range
(D) median and the interquartile range
(E) median and the range

Answer

14. In a high school there are 638 underclassmen (9th and 10th graders) and 523 upperclassmen (11th and 12th graders). Of the underclassmen 83.1% take the bus to school, and of the upperclassmen 70.9% take the bus to school. If a student is chosen at random from those students who take the bus to school, what is the probability that this student is an underclassman?

(A) 0.457   (B) 0.550   (C) 0.588   (D) 0.671   (E) 0.831

Answer

15. A survey is conducted to compare the proportions of men and women who access their bank statements online. Denoting the population proportions by p_M and p_W, a two-proportion z-test is carried out to test $H_0: p_M = p_W$ against $H_a: p_M > p_W$. The value of the test statistic is found to be $z = 0.784$, and the p-value for the test is found to be 0.216. Which of the following is a correct interpretation of the p-value?

(A)   Given the results of the survey, the probability that $p_M > p_w$ is 0.216.
(B)   Given the results of the survey, the probability that $p_M = p_W$ is 0.216.
(C)   Given that $p_M = p_W$, the probability of getting a value of z at least as large as 0.784 is 0.216.
(D)   Given that $p_M > p_W$, the probability of getting a value of z at least as large as 0.784 is 0.216.
(E)   Given that $p_M \neq p_W$, the probability of getting a value of z at least as large as 0.784 is 0.216.

Answer

16. A school district currently allows 12th graders at the high school to drive to school. The Board of Education is considering withdrawing this policy, and wishes to determine the opinions of the parents of students in grades K–12 on the issue.

The Board has a list of email addresses covering the parents of most of the students in the district. An email containing the following message is sent to the parents on the list.

```
Please read the following statement:

"12th graders should not be allowed to drive to
school. The reduction in parking would allow for a
substantial expansion in student activities."

Do you strongly agree, agree, disagree, strongly
disagree, or have no opinion? Please reply with
your response.
```

After three days, the responses are gathered and are analyzed. Which of the following could NOT be considered a source of bias in this study?

(A) The statement is worded in a way that is likely to influence the reader in a particular direction.
(B) The message is sent to parents of students who are not in the 12th grade.
(C) The list of email addresses does not include the parents of all students in the district.
(D) Some parents will not read the email within the three-day period.
(E) Some parents who read the email will choose not to respond.

Answer

17. For a group of students, the correlation between their heights (in inches) and their weights (in pounds) is 0.332. You are given that 1 inch = 2.54 centimeters and that 1 pound = 0.454 kilogram. If the heights are expressed in centimeters and the weights are expressed in kilograms, what will be the value of the correlation?

(A) 0.059   (B) 0.288   (C) 0.332   (D) 0.383   (E) 1.857

Answer

18. A track and field coach has observed two javelin throwers for a long period of time, and now has to select one of them for the team. Which of the following would NOT be a good reason to choose thrower A in preference to B?

(A) The mean for thrower A is greater than the mean for thrower B.
(B) The median for thrower A is greater than the median for thrower B.
(C) The third quartile for thrower A is greater than the third quartile for thrower B.
(D) The maximum for thrower A is greater than the maximum for thrower B.
(E) The distribution of A's throws is positively skewed whereas the distribution of B's throws is roughly symmetrical.

Answer

19. A company is developing a new drug for reducing the symptoms of pollen allergies. They have developed two forms of the drug: A and B. The company wants to find out which form of the drug is most effective and to determine whether the amount to be taken each day should be split into one, two, or three doses. A set of volunteers who suffer from pollen allergies is split into six groups to receive treatments according to the following table.

	1 Dose	2 Doses	3 Doses
Drug A			
Drug B			

How many explanatory variables (factors) are there in this experiment?

(A) 1   (B) 2   (C) 3   (D) 5   (E) 6

Answer

20. An airline observes a random sample of its flights on a particular route. The 95% confidence interval for the mean time (in minutes) for all flights on this route is calculated to be (47.0, 53.0). Which of the following is NOT true?

(A) At the 95% confidence level, the true mean flight time is within 3.0 minutes of the sample mean flight time.

(B) If the true mean flight time were outside the interval (47.0, 53.0) then the sample mean that was found would be very unlikely.

(C) Approximately $2\frac{1}{2}$% of flights on this route are longer than 53 minutes.

(D) We are 95% confident that the true mean flight time is between 47.0 and 53.0 minutes.

(E) If many random samples of the same size were taken and the 95% confidence intervals were calculated, then 95% of the confidence intervals would contain the true mean flight time.

Answer

21. A "population" is formed by placing five balls in a bag. The balls are labeled 1, 2, 3, 4, and 5, respectively. The mean of this population is $\mu = 3$. Someone who does not know the contents of the bag will estimate the value of μ by randomly taking a sample of three of the balls (without replacement) and finding <u>either</u> the sample mean <u>or</u> the sample median.

In the meantime, a statistician has listed all the possible samples of size three (sampling without replacement) and has calculated the sample mean and the sample median for each possible sample. The statistician finds that:

- All the possible sample <u>means</u> form a distribution whose mean is 3 and whose standard deviation is 0.577.
- All the possible sample <u>medians</u> form a distribution whose mean is 3 and whose standard deviation is 0.775.

Regarding the choice between using the sample mean and using the sample median for estimating μ, which of the following is true?

(A) Both the sample mean and the sample median are unbiased, but the sample median is preferable as it has the larger standard deviation.
(B) Both the sample mean and the sample median are unbiased, but the sample mean is preferable as it has the smaller standard deviation.
(C) The sample mean is unbiased and the sample median is biased, so the sample mean is preferable.
(D) The sample median is unbiased and the sample mean is biased, so the sample median is preferable.
(E) Both the sample mean and the sample median are biased.

Answer

22. A set of cards cards consists of 12 red cards (numbered 1–12), 12 purple cards (numbered 1–12), 12 green cards (numbered 1–12), and 12 yellow cards (numbered 1–12). One card is going to be picked at random. Let A be the event that the card is green and let B be the event that the card is a 12. Which of the following is true?

(A) The events A and B are independent and mutually exclusive.
(B) The events A and B are independent but not mutually exclusive.
(C) The events A and B are not independent but are mutually exclusive.
(D) The events A and B are not independent and not mutually exclusive.
(E) It is not possible to tell from the information given whether or not the events A and B are mutually exclusive.

Answer

23. A new warm-up procedure has been suggested for use before working out, and it is hoped that the procedure will encourage a greater increase in muscle mass. In order to test this, a study is designed using 40 volunteers who already work out regularly.

The volunteers will be randomly split into two groups, each of size 20. The first group will be taught the warm-up exercises and will be supervised doing the exercises prior to their regular workouts. The second group will merely continue with their regular workouts. At the beginning and at the end of the study, the muscle mass of each of the volunteers will be measured by people who do not know which volunteers were in which group.

Which of the following is NOT the case in the study described?

(A) This study is an experiment.
(B) Randomization is used.
(C) A control group is used.
(D) The study is conducted in a double-blind manner.
(E) There is no blocking involved in the study.

Answer

24. A set of scores has mean 70.3 and a standard deviation 8.8. The scores are now scaled according to the formula $y = 0.7x + 30$, where x is the old score and y is the new score. What is the standard deviation of the new scores?

(A) 4.31   (B) 6.16   (C) 7.36   (D) 36.16   (E) 37.36

Answer

25. In a high school, all of the 11th graders take both math and physics. After the students have taken the midyear exam in both subjects, the physics teachers are considering the results, and have found the value of r^2, the square of the correlation coefficient between the math scores and the physics scores. Which of the following is best answered by consideration of the value of r^2 ?

(A)   Whether high physics scores are associated with high math scores
(B)   Whether the relationship between physics scores and math scores would be better represented by a curve or a straight line
(C)   To what extent the variation in physics scores can be explained by a linear relationship between physics scores and math scores
(D)   Whether there is an outlier in the scatterplot of physics scores and math scores
(E)   Whether the physics scores are on the whole higher than the math scores

Answer

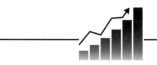

26. In a random sample of 400 adults, each person stated his or her political preference. The sex (male/female) of each respondent was also noted. The results are shown in the table below.

	Democrat	Republican	Other
Male	94	78	18
Female	88	86	36

If political preference is independent of sex, which of the following is the expected number of respondents who are female and support the Democratic Party?

(A) 40.04   (B) 46.20   (C) 86.45   (D) 95.55   (E) 103.895

Answer

27. Suppose that an observational study has shown that people who regularly consume substantial amounts of olive oil live longer lives, on average, than those who do not. Of the following arguments, which is strongest in explaining why the result of the study does <u>not</u> imply that in order to live longer one should start to regularly consume substantial amounts of olive oil?

(A) Olive oil is high in fat, and it's not a good idea to eat high-fat foods.
(B) There are many other factors contributing to how long you live that were not considered by the study.
(C) If a person is recorded as eating substantial amounts of olive oil and living a long life, we don't know whether the long life was caused by the olive oil eating or, for example, regular exercise.
(D) People who choose to include substantial amounts of olive oil in their diets might well be the sort of people who have healthier lifestyles in general, and a healthy lifestyle leads to a long life.
(E) Olive oil is associated with frying, and frying is unhealthy.

Answer

28. A team of psychologists is studying the behavior of the students in a first grade class. There are 16 girls and 16 boys in the class, and for each student the psychologists record the number of minutes "on task" during a forty minute class. The team wishes to compare the on-task times of the girls with the on-task times of the boys. Which of the following would NOT be a suitable graph for displaying the results?

(A) Parallel dotplots with equal scales
(B) Back-to-back stemplot
(C) Histograms with equal scales
(D) Side-by-side boxplots
(E) Scatterplot with girls' times plotted as x-values and boys' times plotted as y-values

Answer

29. The amount of flour per bag delivered by a machine is known to have a standard deviation of 0.4 ounce. What is the minimum sample size required to estimate the mean amount of flour per bag to within 0.1 ounce with 95% confidence?

(A) 3　　　(B) 8　　　(C) 43　　　(D) 62　　　(E) 154

Answer

30. In the context of z- and t-tests for the mean using small samples, which of the following is (are) true?

      I. The z-test requires the assumption that the population distribution is normal.
     II. The t-test requires the assumption that the population distribution is normal.
    III. The t-test is used when the population standard deviation is unknown.

(A) I only
(B) I and II only
(C) I and III only
(D) II and III only
(E) I, II, and III

Answer

31. When a large number of a particular type of seed is planted, it is known that 70% of the seeds will germinate. In addition, the germination of any one seed is independent of the germination of any other seed. If 20 of the seeds are planted, what are the mean and the standard deviation of the number of seeds that germinate?

(A) mean = 0.7, standard deviation = 0.102
(B) mean = 0.7, standard deviation = 0.458
(C) mean = 14, standard deviation = 0.102
(D) mean = 14, standard deviation = 2.049
(E) mean = 14, standard deviation = 4.2

Answer

32. A company has a machine that produces cans of coconut milk, and it has been noticed that the amount of coconut milk varies from can to can. The amounts are normally distributed with standard deviation 8 milliliters. The label used on the cans states that each can contains 414 milliliters. The management of the company decides to set the mean μ of the amount of coconut milk per can so that 98% of the cans contain more than 414 milliliters. Of the following, which is the closest to the amount (in milliliters) to which μ should be set?

(A) 395.4   (B) 397.6   (C) 421.8   (D) 430.4   (E) 432.6

Answer

33. A political party wishes to estimate the proportion of voters that support the party in a particular state. The party will poll a random sample of n voters from the state. Which of the following is likely to result in the smallest margin of error?

(A) $n = 400$, confidence level = 95%
(B) $n = 400$, confidence level = 98%
(C) $n = 400$, confidence level = 99%
(D) $n = 500$, confidence level = 95%
(E) $n = 500$, confidence level = 99%

Answer

34. A pharmaceutical company wishes to compare the effectiveness of three drugs, A, B, and C, that are designed to reduce blood pressure. The company believes that the younger a person is, the more likely he is to respond to a drug of this sort. The company intends to design an experiment in which each subject will be instructed to take one of the drugs regularly for a four week period. Each subject's blood pressure will be measured at the beginning and at the end of the four week period.

There are three young men, three middle-aged men, and three elderly men available to take part in this study. Which of the following is the most appropriate method for assigning the treatment groups?

(A) For each man, randomly choose which drug he will be given.
(B) From the whole set of nine men, randomly choose three to receive drug A, three to receive B, and three to receive C.
(C) For the three young men, randomly assign one man to drug A, one man to drug B, and one man to drug C; repeat this process for the middle-aged men and for the elderly men.
(D) Randomly choose one of the drugs, and give that drug to all the young men; randomly choose one of the remaining drugs and give that to all the middle-aged men; and then give the third drug to all the elderly men.
(E) Randomly pick one man from each age group and from these three randomly assign one to drug A, one to drug B, and one to drug C; then pick another man from each age group and do the same thing; then do the same thing for the remaining three men.

Answer

35. A manufacturer of tires has used a particular type of rubber for a long time, and has established over the years that the mean life of the tires is 40,000 miles. However, the company has now changed the type of rubber used and needs to find out whether the mean life of the tires has changed. Having tested a random sample of the tires, a t-test for the mean is carried out using H_0: $\mu = 40,000$ *versus* H_a: $\mu \neq 40,000$. The t-value for the test is found to be -1.902 and the p-value is found to be 0.063. Using a 5% significance level, which of the following is a correct conclusion for the test?

   (A) Since $p > 0.05$ we do not have sufficient evidence to conclude that the mean life of the tires is not equal to 40,000 miles.
   (B) Since $p > 0.05$ we do not have sufficient evidence to conclude that the mean life of the tires is less than 40,000 miles.
   (C) Since $p > 0.05$ we have sufficient evidence to conclude that the mean life of the tires is equal to 40,000 miles.
   (D) Since $p > 0.05$ we have sufficient evidence to conclude that the mean life of the tires is not equal to 40,000 miles.
   (E) Since $p > 0.05$ we have sufficient evidence to conclude that the mean life of the tires is greater than 40,000 miles.

Answer

36. A very large population has standard deviation denoted by σ. A random sample of size n will be taken from this population. The quantity $\dfrac{\sigma}{\sqrt{n}}$ is

   (A) the mean of the distribution of the sample standard deviation
   (B) the standard deviation of the sampling distribution of the sample mean
   (C) the standard deviation of the sample
   (D) an estimate of the population standard deviation
   (E) an estimate of the sample standard deviation calculated from the population standard deviation

Answer

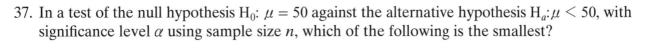
37. In a test of the null hypothesis H_0: $\mu = 50$ against the alternative hypothesis H_a: $\mu < 50$, with significance level α using sample size n, which of the following is the smallest?

(A) The probability of Type II error when $\mu = 48$, given that $n = 40$ and $\alpha = 0.05$

(B) The probability of Type II error when $\mu = 46$, given that $n = 40$ and $\alpha = 0.05$

(C) The probability of Type II error when $\mu = 48$, given that $n = 40$ and $\alpha = 0.01$

(D) The probability of Type II error when $\mu = 46$, given that $n = 40$ and $\alpha = 0.01$

(E) The probability of Type II error when $\mu = 48$, given that $n = 20$ and $\alpha = 0.05$

Answer

38. Having graded a test, a teacher was interested in the relationship between the amount of time the students studied for the test and the scores they received. She asked the 24 students individually how much they studied, and then compiled a list giving for each student the amount of time studied and the score on the test. The teacher performed a least squares regression analysis. Part of the computer output from that analysis is shown below.

```
Dependent variable: Score on test

Predictor          Coef      SE Coef          T          P
Constant      69.555194     3.721432      18.69     <.0001
Time           0.2642443    0.109216       2.42     0.0243

S = 6.3241      R-sq = 21.0%    R-sq (adj) = 17.5%
```

Which of the following is a 99% confidence interval for the slope of the regression line that relates the time spent studying and the score on the test?

(A) $69.555 \pm (2.807)(3.721)$
(B) $69.555 \pm (2.819)(3.721)$
(C) $69.555 \pm (18.69)(3.721)$
(D) $0.264 \pm (2.807)(0.109)$
(E) $0.264 \pm (2.819)(0.109)$

Answer

39. Every afternoon, Jennifer waits for a subway train. The density curve for the amount of time she has to wait (in minutes) is shown in the diagram below.

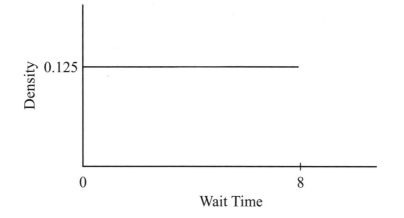

The mean and standard deviation of the wait time are 4 and 2.309, respectively. If a random sample of 40 afternoons is taken, what is the approximate probability that Jennifer's sample mean wait time is less than 5 minutes?

(A) 0.003
(B) 0.332
(C) 0.625
(D) 0.668
(E) 0.997

Answer

40. Two variables, x and y, were measured for a random sample of 10 subjects. In the first of two transformations, log y was plotted (on the vertical axis) against x (on the horizontal axis), a least squares regression was performed on the transformed variables, and the following residual plot was obtained.

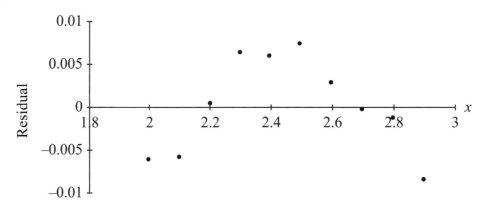

In the second transformation, log y was plotted (on the vertical axis) against log x (on the horizontal axis), a least squares regression was performed on the transformed variables, and the following residual plot was obtained.

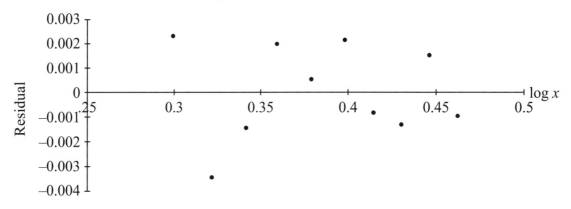

Which of the following conclusions is best supported by the evidence above?

(A) x and y are related according to an equation of the form $y = ax^p$, where a and p are constants.

(B) x and y are related according to an equation of the form $y = a + x^p$, where a and p are constants.

(C) x and y are related according to an equation of the form $y = a \cdot b^x$, where a and b are constants.

(D) x and y are related according to an equation of the form $y = a + b^x$, where a and b are constants.

(E) x and y are related according to an equation of the form $y = a + b \log x$, where a and b are constants.

Answer

SECTION II PART A

Questions 1–5
Spend about 65 minutes on this part of the exam.
Percent of Section II grade—75

Directions: Show all your work. Indicate clearly the methods you use, because you will be graded on the correctness of your method as well as on the accuracy and completeness of your results and explanations.

1. For several years, Ellen has been recording music onto audio cassettes. Having accumulated 81 cassettes in this way, she has recently had all of them transferred to digital format, with each cassette going over to one computer file. The sizes of these 81 files in megabytes (MB) are summarized in the table below.

N	MEAN	MEDIAN	STDEV	SE MEAN	MIN	MAX	Q1	Q3
81	544.78	566	167.26	18.58	99	774	463	667.5

(a) Are there any outliers in this data set? Show clearly the method you use to answer this question.

(b) Based on the information given, do you think that the distribution of the file sizes is skewed to the right, skewed to the left, or roughly symmetrical? Explain your answer.

(c)   Approximately what percent of the computer files have sizes between 463 and 667.5 megabytes? Explain.

(d)   The standard deviation is given as 167.26. Explain how this value summarizes the variability of the file sizes.

2. A driver is interested in buying a new car of a particular type, and she wants to find out how the value of the car is likely to change in its first few years. She randomly selects 20 used cars of this type that are for sale and are at least one year and at most three years old, and notes for each its age (in years) and its price (in dollars). She then uses a computer to fit a least squares regression line to the data. Part of the computer output is shown below.

```
Dependent variable: Price

Predictor         Coef      SE Coef        T          P
Constant      25844.789    1073.413     24.08     <.0001
Age           -4764.155    526.3235     -9.05     <.0001

S = 1498.81      R-sq = 82.0%    R-sq (adj) = 81.0%
```

(a) What is the value of the correlation coefficient for age and price? Interpret this correlation.

(b) State the equation of the regression line and interpret its slope in the context of this question.

(c) State and interpret the value of the intercept of the regression line. Can this value be usefully applied to the prices of this type of car?

When the driver used the computer to fit the least squares regression line to the data, the computer also displayed the residual plot shown below.

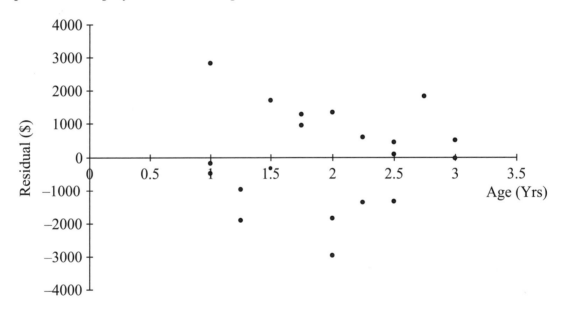

(d) What does the residual plot tell you about the appropriateness of using the least squares regression line to model the prices of cars of this type that are at least one year and at most three years old? Explain.

3. An investor is trying to decide between two mutual funds, Fund A and Fund B. The investor consults an economist, who estimates that for either of the two funds the amount of money gained in any given month on a $1000 dollar investment is approximately normally distributed, and that the gain or loss in any month can be considered to be independent of the gain or loss in any other month. Moreover, the economist estimates that, if the current economic climate continues, the monthly gains on $1000 in the two funds have the expected values (means) and standard deviations given in the table below.

Gain in dollars on a $1000 investment

	Expected Value	Standard Deviation
Fund A	4	5
Fund B	4	18

Assume throughout this question that the current economic climate continues.

(a) Explain why the investor might choose Fund A over Fund B.

(b) In any given month, what is the probability that Fund A gains money?

(c)   What is the probability that Fund A gains money in exactly two of the next four months?

(d)   A different investor decides to invest $8000 in Fund A and $3000 in Fund B. Assuming that the amounts gained by the two funds are independent, what are the mean and the standard deviation of the amount gained by this investment in the first month?

4. A company is developing a new treatment for gloves worn by gymnasts. The hope is that this treatment will more effectively prevent wear on the gloves than the treatment in use for gloves currently on the market. The company will recruit 50 male gymnasts as volunteers who will wear the gloves as they usually would for six months.

An employee at the company suggests an experimental design whereby the 50 gymnasts would be randomly assigned to two groups of 25. One group would be given gloves with the new treatment and the other would be given gloves with the current treatment. At the end of the study the wear on the gloves with the new treatment would be compared to the wear on the gloves with the current treatment.

(a) How would you assign the 50 gymnasts to the two groups of 25 for a completely randomized design?

(b) Why would the groups be assigned randomly rather than, for example, allowing some of the gymnasts to choose which group they would be in?

The company employs a statistician who suggests a different experimental design. Each of the gymnasts will be given a pair of gloves of which one glove has been treated with the new treatment and the other has been treated with the current treatment. For each gymnast it will be randomly decided whether it is the left glove or the right glove that receives the new treatment.

(c)　Explain why this second experimental design is preferable to the first.

5. An experiment was designed to determine whether, in a test of physical endurance, the presence of other participants improved performance. The 32 students in a high school class were randomly assigned to two groups: Group 1 and Group 2. Each student was asked to hold a weight at arm's length in his or her dominant hand for as long as possible. The time (in seconds) for which each student was able to continue to hold the weight in this way was noted. (The same weight was used for each student, and care was taken to ensure that the students' arms were straight, and held in a horizontal position to the side of the body.) Each student in Group 1 performed the task with only the time recorder present. When students in Group 2 performed the task, the other students in Group 2 remained in the room and were allowed to give encouragement to the person performing the task.

The following results were obtained.

Group 1	180	128	135	207	120	207	159	187	183	83	53	154	72	128	105	227
Group 2	278	126	258	280	225	216	166	138	177	162	301	199	76	390	145	384

Does the presence of other participants appear to bring about a higher mean time for this task? Give appropriate statistical evidence to support your conclusion.

SECTION II PART B

Question 6
Spend about 25 minutes on this part of the exam.
Percent of Section II grade—25

Directions: Show all your work. Indicate clearly the methods you use, because you will be graded on the correctness of your method as well as on the accuracy and completeness of your results and explanations.

6. A Board of Education is considering changing the schedule at its two high schools, Central and Northern, so that the school day will start and end one hour later than it does currently. In order to get an idea of student attitudes about the idea, the Board instructs each school to perform a survey on a small sample of its student body.

   (a) The administration of Central High School selects a random sample of 40 students at the school and asks each student in the sample whether or not he/she is in favor of the idea. Twenty-six of the students respond that they are in favor, and the remaining 14 students respond that they are not in favor. Perform a test to determine whether this result provides evidence that a majority of the students at Central High School are in favor of the idea.

The administration of Northern High School decides to include in its survey the possibility of "No Opinion." It designs the following survey question.

> "The school day should start and end one hour later."
>
> Disagree (D) _____   No opinion (N) _____   Agree (A) _____

The administration decides that a "D" will score 0, an "N" will score 1, and an "A" will score 2. Having administered the survey to a random sample of 20 students, the administration adds up the scores and finds a total score of 24. An assistant is now given the job of using simulation in order to facilitate a decision as to whether this result reflects support for the idea amongst the student body of Northern High School as a whole. Parts (b), (c), and (d) of this question are concerned with this process.

(b)   Suppose that the three responses are favored by equal proportions of students at Northern High School. How would you assign digits in a random number table to simulate the responses to this survey?

(c) Use the random number table given below and your assignment of digits from part (b) to simulate the responses from one sample of 20 students. Show your work clearly on the table, and note the total score for your sample.

4	4	7	3	8	8	5	3	5	1	7	7	6	7	8
6	3	7	6	4	2	5	9	3	9	5	3	8	8	9
6	6	4	8	5	2	5	2	9	9	4	6	9	8	8
1	6	9	0	9	9	0	1	0	4	9	7	4	8	0

The assistant runs the simulation in part (c) 200 times, and obtains the following results.

Total Score	10	11	12	13	14	15	16	17	18	19	20	21	22	23	24	25	26	27	28	29	30
Number of Runs	1	3	4	3	8	9	16	13	26	11	17	15	28	16	15	6	5	2	0	1	1

(d) On the basis of this set of results (which is based on the assumption that the three responses are favored by equal proportions of the school), do you think that a total score of 24 in a sample of 20 students gives convincing evidence that the student body as a whole is in favor of the idea? Explain carefully the logic behind your answer.

INDEX
for Multiple-Choice Questions

Roman numerals in bold face type represent sample exam numbers. Other numbers are question numbers.